A
GREAT CLOUD
OF WITNESSES

BOOK I

20 BIOGRAPHIES

BY: DR. ED REESE

Faith Baptist Church Publications
3794 Oleander Avenue
Fort Pierce, Florida 34982
1996
Fourth Printing 2003

WHY BIOGRAPHIES?

1. Biographies have always been used of God to stimulate more service for Christ. Paul said, "Be ye followers of me as I am also of Christ." Only eternity will reveal how many have gone into Christian service or a deeper walk with God as a result of reading such as David Brainerd's journal.

2. Biographies keep the wonderful ministries of many people alive and fresh before us. Many might soon be forgotten unless their challenging stories are brought to the attention f the Christian world afresh.

3. Biographies introduce people to us whom we might not know, or perhaps have misunderstood. This would be especially true of people now living. In a day when Christians seem to be divided into many "camps", it is hoped that this series will help give all true believers a new appreciation of ministries other than their own.

4. Biographies introduces us to people we will soon be living with for all eternity. The "family of God" is such a wonderful family. If you do not have that assurance that heaven is your home, that your sins have been forgiven, and that Jesus Christ lives in and through your life, please write us. We would like to introduce you to the Saviour, and welcome you to this wonderful eternal family.

ED REESE, Psalm 35:28

Printed by permission of Ed Reese
Faith Baptist Church Publications
3794 Oleander Avenue
Fort Pierce, Florida 34982
Copyright 1996
Reprinted 1999
Third Printing 2002

CONTENTS

The Life
And Ministry Of

Hyman Jedidiah Appelman
1902

HYMAN JEDIDIAH APPELMAN

BORN: January 7, 1902
DIED:
Moghiliev, (White) Russia

In the past fifty years there have been few evangelists whose ministry has been as effective, far reaching and productive as that of this converted Jew. He actually helped spear-head the modern day swing to mass evangelism, as his city-wide endeavors in the early forties whipped up enthusiasm for evangelism that was all but forgotten since the era of Billy Sunday, Mordecai Ham and Bob Jones, Sr.

He was born on the banks of the Dnieper River in White Russia of Orthodox Jewish parents. He was reared and trained in the Jewish faith by a strict grandfather and grandmother. One time as a boy he was thrown from a horse with the horse stamping on him and almost killing him. For days he wore a kind of strait jacket. He always remembered the day it was taken off and what a relief that was. He later described his salvation experience as the same type of relief from the bondage of sin.

His father had come to America one and a half years prior to the rest of the family. Arriving with his mother and three younger brothers in December 1914, Hyman knew Hebrew, and had a fair command of German, Russian, Yiddish and Polish. Now, he had to learn English. He was enrolled in the Hans Christian Andersen Public School in Chicago. He was a thirteen year old boy weighing almost 150 pounds and had to sit in one of the small first grade seats. Despite the handicap of learning a new language, he went through the first eight grades in two years with high marks, then went on to preparatory school.

Eventually he enrolled at Northwestern University where he received his A.B. Degree, and also at DePaul University where he received his LL.B. Degree, attending both schools from 1918-1921. He graduated from DePaul University as one of the highest in the class and was awarded a scholarship. He received his license to practice law in 1921 and was a successful trial lawyer in Chicago from 1921 to 1925. The two year scholarship that he received allowed him to attend evening classes, and in those three years (1921-1923) he received his LL.M. Degree. In 1922 one of the professors at DePaul University died and Appelman was invited to teach his academy classes. Thus he was teaching school, attending school, and practicing law. His father was now in a building business and turned over his legal business to his son. At this time, Appelman was not very religious, although he was not what you would call irreligious or non-religious. He belonged to a synagogue, attended three times a year, was engaged to marry a young Jewish girl, did not drink or gamble, but had no contact with the New Testament. This type of life produced a discontented unhappiness in his heart for which he could find no satisfaction. He tried to drown it in work and more work.

6

In the fall of 1924 he almost had a breakdown. He was finally able to go back to the office on a limited basis. One night when he came home, he found a conference with father, mother, brother, law partner and family doctor who said that he had to take a vacation. He decided he would like to go West and left in December 1924.

His first destination was Kansas City. He checked in the YMCA intending to see Rabbai Silbert in a day or two. Being Saturday (Jewish holiday), he was in the lobby of the YMCA and joined in an argument that lasted from about 4 to 10 p.m. Later that night an elderly man knocked on his door and introduced himself as Daly, a reporter of the *Kansas City Star*. He had been in the argument downstairs. For one hour he witnessed about Christ to Appelman. He left after he got Appelman to promise to read the New Testament. Hyman saw a Gideon Bible and opened it. Once in Chicago, he remembered walking by a street meeting and remembered one phrase as he had walked by rapidly, "if a man wanted religion in a hurry, he should read John." Appelman, assuming it must be somewhere in the New Testament, found it and read it about five times. At 8 a.m. someone knocked at the door and a Mr. Garrett asked him to go to Sunday School with him. He didn't have the heart to say no, so attended the Institutional Methodist Church in Kansas City. After it was over, Garrett said, "Would you mind staying for church?" Appelman agreed and attended his first Protestant Church service of any kind. He had been to a few Catholic services previously and was surprised to see no decorations, pictures, statues, crosses, holy water, robes, quiet organ music and his thought was: Don't these people have any religion at all? He had never seen a choir loft, a big pulpit Bible, a preacher without a robe. He endured the service, although it made no sense to him. He then went to the Rabbai's home.

Hyman traveled with several members of this family to visit other kinfolk in St. Louis, in Kansas City, and then on to Omaha and Denver in March 1925. He dropped from 213 to 151 pounds in less than four months. He saw one of the secretaries, Mr. Durrett, at the local YMCA where he was staying and asked where he could find a good doctor. The secretary said he couldn't help him but told him about his church across the street, Central Christian Church of Denver and the pastor, Dr. James E. Davis, and advised him to counsel with him. This was the largest Christian church in the Disciples of Christ denomination of that time.

Appelman crossed the street and met Davis. The conversation started at about 3 p.m. and lasted past midnight. Finally, Dr. Davis told him: "You don't need a doctor, my boy, you need the Lord Jesus Christ!" Davis, thoroughly explained the whole truth of the Saviour and Appelman drank it in. The preacher dropped to his knees, put his arm around Appelman and began to pray with a tender, broken voice, great tears coursing down his cheeks. The devil was losing the fight. The battle was mostly centered around the fact that his parents, four brothers and sister would have their hearts broken, but the preacher refused to surrender his soul to the enemy.

Appelman asked for Romans 10:9 to be explained, and finally through clenched teeth, he said, "Lord, I do not know and I do not understand, but this man says and this Book says that Your Son died for my sins, and that if I ask You to, for His sake, You will forgive my sins. Lord, for Jesus' sake, do forgive my sins."

The two stood to their feet, and Appelman said, "What must I do next?" Baptism was discussed and was agreed upon for the next Sunday morning. He and another young man came forward to publicly confess Christ and he was baptized. He walked to the nearest Western Union Office and sent a telegram home, "I'm a Christian, I've been baptized, I've joined the church, I'm praying for you." He was twenty-three years old. A reply came back the same day, "Come on home." During that week he received at least a dozen telegrams and letters. The next week his sweetheart came. She refused to stay in Denver so went back to Chicago thus ending their engagement.

His conversion naturally had created a stir in Jewish circles, and he became an outcast from his family. He wanted to stay in Denver to learn more about the Bible before going back to a confrontation with his kin folk. Staying in Denver until August and finding odd jobs to support himself, he began to give his testimony and preach. The first Sunday in August he preached the morning and evening messages in the church where he was converted while the pastor was on vacation. That night he received a telegram from home saying his mother was dying. He took the first train home. The father had faked the message to get Hyman home and to plead with him to reconsider his ways. When Appelman refused, the father with indignation and wrath said, "When your sides come together from hunger and you come crawling to my door, I will throw you a crust of bread as I would any other dog."

Appelman took the first train East. He got a job with the Reading Railroad in Camden, New Jersey; but things did not go well and he began to backslide. He worked there until November 1925, then decided to come back to Chicago and commit suicide by swimming out into Lake Michigan as far as he could, then just drown. At Pittsburgh there was a lay-over between trains. Walking the streets he saw a recruiting sign of the United States Army on the front of the Post Office building. Hyman decided to enlist on the spot thinking this might give him an alternative to ending it all. He was sent to Walter Reed Hospital in Washington, D.C., where he was to serve in the medical department for three years, and arrived on Sunday. He went to a building marked "YMCA Hut" and, walking in the wrong door, found himself in the parlor where a Mr. Howard, the "Y" secretary was teaching a Sunday School class. He told Mr. Howard his story and was soon introduced to the chaplain, a Lutheran preacher. The chaplain got him interested in teaching a class at the large Gospel Mission in Washington. It was at this mission he met the girl, Verna Cook, who later became his wife. She was teaching a class of girls. He was promoted and made a staff sergeant, worked for a while with the sick and wounded officers, then was made mess sergeant. Discharged, he had no place to go, so he re-enlisted for a second term in the service. He was sent to a station hospital in Fort Sill, Oklahoma, near Lawton. He transferred his membership from the Temple Baptist Church in Washington to the Central Baptist Church of Lawton in December 1927, and began to teach in Sunday

School. By November 1928, Appelman was preaching, sometimes in uniform and sometimes in civilian clothes. He held a revival meeting near Lawton in a little schoolhouse called Woodlawn. Every unsaved person in that entire district was converted, the church was reorganized, and Appelman was called to be the pastor. This was in March 1930.

Because the Southern Baptists do not accept alien immersion, he was baptized again and ordained May 30 at the Central Baptist Church of Lawton, Oklahoma, pastored by S. R. McClung. When hands were laid on him, he surrendered everything he had to the Lord and purchased his discharge from the Army in August 1930.

On September 4, 1930, he married Verna Cook, of Livermore Falls, Maine. Feeling a definite call to the ministry, he went to Southwestern Baptist Theological Seminary in Fort Worth, Texas, from 1930 to 1933, where he received his theological training. His wife attended the same seminary and has an M.D. degree in Religion Education. Appelman later received an honorary D.D. degree from the Western Baptist Theological Seminary of Portland, Oregon. In addition to his small church at Woodlawn, he was called to be a pastor of another church nearby and pastored both from September 1930 until April 1931. This meant he drove 190 miles each weekend except when he was in revival meetings elsewhere. In April 1931, he held a revival in the Baptist Church of Vickery, Texas. A short time after that the pastor resigned, and Appelman was called to head up the work. He pastored there until May of 1934.

It was in December 1933 that Dr. J. Howard Williams, the State Secretary for the Texas Baptist Convention, told him that he was elected to be one of the State Evangelists for Texas. He held that position until January of 1942, faithfully ministering for eight years in End on End Crusades for the Southern Baptist Convention. However, as he was becoming nationally known, he felt the call of God for a larger ministry. Resigning, he launched into single church meetings, co-operative campaigns, city and country-wide crusades, across the country, and soon was spending some time each year in a foreign country.

In January 1942, he held his first large crusade in Philadelphia, Pennsylvania, where, at the invitation of more than 200 churches, he preached for three weeks in Town Hall and later in Convention Hall. Under the organizing guidance of Horace Dean, the meetings brought salvation to some 2,700 in the three week crusade, with total decisions of all kinds over the 5,000 figure. In 1944, he was in a great tent revival in Los Angeles, California, sponsored by the various churches and Christian Business Men's Committees of that area. Crowds numbered 7,000 to 8,000 with 2,500 conversions in the three week crusade. In 1948 (January 11-February 1) in Detroit, Michigan, he had 2,700 professions of faith in a city-wide endeavor. Other memorable crusades included Danville, Illinois, in March of 1950 with 1,061 first time decisions in two weeks, followed by a good San Francisco, California, meeting. In Decatur, Illinois, in 1951 there were 3,300 decisions in three weeks. After preaching a devastating sermon against Communism one night in Decatur, his tent was burned down. This helped to bring out a crowd of 6,000 for the next service. In Portsmouth, Virginia, 1964, he had 1,700 professions of faith in a three week city-wide endeavor. He has conducted over 25 crusades in the city of Dallas alone. Many have been conducted in Fort Worth and at least a dozen in Houston, Texas. At least fifteen revivals have been conducted in Oklahoma City, Oklahoma. Over 50 crusades have been held in California, including Stockton and Oakland crusades. City-wide crusades have been conducted in such places as Mobile and Montgomery, Alabama; Phoenix, Arizona; Denver, Colorado; Tampa and St. Petersburg, Florida; Rockford, Illinois; Evansville, Gary and Hammond, Indiana; Louisville, Kentucky; Grand Rapids, Kalamazoo, Lansing and Holland, Michigan; St. Louis, Missouri; Cleveland, Ohio; Portland, Oregon; Altoona, Pennsylvania; Bristol, Tennessee; El Paso, Texas; Lynchburg, Virginia; and Seattle, Washington, to name just a few.

His overseas ministries have taken him to such places as Australia in 1948, where for six months with song evangelist, Homer Britton, a mighty revival took place. Some 9,600 professions of faith were witnessed in some of the largest auditoriums of the land. He spent three months in 1951 in Great Britain, and some time in Mexico City, Mexico, in 1952 with 200 being saved the first night of the crusade there. In 1955 he saw some 3,000 decisions made in a Guatemala campaign with crowds of 3,000 to 7,000 attending nightly. In 1957 he returned to the land of his birth to preach, which took him to a number of places in the Soviet Union. In 1959, he conducted campaigns in Northern Ireland, Greece, Portugal, Spain, Germany, France, Holland and Russia. In 1960 he saw 1,350 first time decisions in a one month ministry in Mexico City and Pachuca, Mexico. In 1962 there were 3,700 decisions in 23 days in Dominica and Trinidad. In 1969-70 (December-February) he saw 5,879 first time decisions in the states of Madras and Kerala in India. In the fifties he also ministered in Germany, Poland, Costa Rica, Finland, Nicaragua, Switzerland, Sweden and Canada. In the sixties such places as Korea, Japan, Israel, Syria, Taiwan, Egypt, Jordan, Indonesia, Singapore, and Hong Kong were visited.

He has been eight times around the world and has made three trips to Russia as an evangelist - in 1957, 1959 and 1963.

His 40th year of evangelistic meetings in 1974 had 48 campaigns in nineteen states. He spent 51 weeks of the year on the road. The test of a competent evangelist is being invited back to be with those whom he had been with previously, and Appelman always has a good share of repeat meetings like this. Decisions this year were 9,809, with 4,158 uniting for church membership.

His schedule of meetings leaves one breathless. It is hard to find a day in the last 45 years that he has not been preaching somewhere. An average Appelman year will see some 7,000 first time professions of faith. By 1969 he had seen over 345,000 total decisions for Christ, with some 270,000 uniting with churches and over 125,000 rededications by Christians. With the day of city-wide crusades waning, the last several years have found Appelman being that of a local church evangelist, with the results in single church meetings continuing just as large.

He has had numerous song leaders such Homer Britton, Chelsea Stockwell, Stratton Shufelt, John Troy, Garland Cofield, and Ellis Zehr, traveling with him.

Ellis Zehr recalls some of the blessings of his association from 1959 to 1964. He states that wherever Appelman has gone, men have turned to Christ through his ministry. He has been able to communicate well even through interpreters. In street meetings in Trinidad people repeated after him in one grand chorus, "Lord, I know I am a sinner and Christ died for me. Save me for Jesus' sake." A pastor in Indianapolis tells that prayer meetings doubled the year following Appelman's meetings. A New York pastor recalls baptizing 100 Appelman converts who continued on in their service for Christ. Besides Zehr's recollections, church after church testify of the increase. Beth Haven Baptist Church of Louisville, Kentucky, reports a week with Appelman produced 198 first time professions; and in the two months following, Sunday School increased by nearly 300. Pastor James Stuart, of the First Baptist Church of Concord, N.H., sums up what most pastors say after Appelman has been to a city.

> "This has been the greatest single week in the 140 years' history of this church. The Appelman meetings have drawn larger crowds, more visitors, have seen more decisions for Christ than any campaign of any kind ever held here. This morning we have more people present than in any one service at any time before."

The fact of the matter is that Appelman does create this kind of a response. His prayer life, hard work and Biblical preaching reminds one of the Apostle Paul.

He is a member of the Red Bridge Baptist Church of Kansas City where he resides. His children are Edgar, born in 1937, and Rebecca, born in 1938.

His forty-two books are published by Zondervan, Revell and Baker. Titles include such as, *Formula for Revival, Ye Must be Born Again, God's Answer to Man's Sin, The Saviour's Invitation, Come Unto Me, Appelman's Sermon Outlines and Illustrations, Will the Circle Be Broken? Effective Outlines and Illustrations, The Gospel of Salvation, Here is Your Revival, Crossing the Deadline*, and others.

In every campaign there has been radio, and in more recent days, TV coverage, at least of the interview type, ranging from 10 minutes to 4 hours.

Appelman has been a guiding force in the ministry of the American Association for Jewish Evangelism, serving as president for a number of years. He also has been president of the Russian-Ukraine Bible Institute of Saskatoon, Sask., Canada, and president of the Hebrew Christian Alliance as well as being a board member of numerous other missionary organizations.

Tributes to his greatness come from such as R.G. Lee:

> "In loyalty to the Bible, in spiritual fervor in seeking the lost for Christ, in effectual preaching of the Gospel with spiritual passion, in the success with the things that most matter in evangelistic effort, Dr. Appelman, comes close to

weighing sixteen ounces to the pound on God's scale."

Lee Roberson adds:

"The first time that I listened to him preach, my heart was stirred by his fervor, zeal, and passion for souls. Through these years I have watched the records of his revival campaigns--for thirty-five years there has been no abatement of his zeal and his concern for the souls of men. He is a true friend, a gracious brother, and a mighty preacher."

Billy Graham concludes:

"Dr. Appelman is one of the greatest and most powerful preachers of the Gospel I have ever listened to. Twenty years ago I used to listen to him preach night after night and made notes on his sermons. Some of my own knowledge and inspiration concerning mass evangelism came from his ministry. Thousands of names are written in the Lamb's Book of Life because Dr. Appelman passed their way."

The Life
And Ministry Of

William Booth
1829- 1912

WILLIAM BOOTH

BORN: April 10, 1829
Nottingham, England

DIED: August 20, 1912
London, England

LIFE SPAN: 83 years, 4 months, 10 days

"Go for souls, and go for the worst!" was the constant cry of William Booth, founder of the Salvation Army. The multitudes in London's slums convinced him he had discovered his life's work and no one ever took the Gospel to the "down and outer" like he did. In 1865 Booth started with only his wife at his side. . .unappreciated by the established churches of his day, ridiculed and jeered by most everyone. His death 47 years later sharply contrasted as 40,000 attended his funeral service, including Queen Mary of England. His "Army," including 21,203 officers and 8,972 societies, was working in 58 countries preaching the Gospel in 34 languages!

William Booth was born of Church of England parents and was "baptized" when he was two days old. His mother was a devout Christian. His father, Samuel, even though he brought in considerable income, had the misfortune to lose money. At thirteen, Booth was apprenticed to a pawnbroker, limiting his education to that of a private tutor from the Methodist Connexion Church. Thus, he was deprived of the advantages of a good common school education and grew up in poverty. His work day was long, sometimes running sixteen hours a day, with very little pay. That same year his father died, accepting Christ on his death bed. This left William and his mother to struggle on in their poverty. In his teens, he was already interested in social reform and longed to do something to alleviate the sufferings of the poor. He joined a civic reform movement but found this full of corruption as well. He had broken from the Church of England and was now attending Wesley Chapel of Nottingham. One night at 11 p.m. on a street coming home from one of the services, he was saved. This was in 1844, when he was fifteen years of age.

A commemorative table marks the spot at the chapel where Booth began to seek the Lord. Many have knelt near it. One was heard saying "O God, do it again. . ."

Soon after Booth's conversion, James Caughey, a spirit-filled American evangelist, visited Nottingham and preached the Wesleyan message of sanctification with great unction and power. This preaching made a great impression on young Booth and kindled in his own heart a great desire to win souls for Christ. Timid for a while, he finally ventured to read the Bible and deliver some comments on the local street corners. Although he was jeered and scorned and bricks were thrown at him, young Booth did not get discouraged. . .this was just a foretaste of the battle ahead of him. At 17 he preached his first sermon and was licensed by the New Wesleyan Connexion.

One day he brought a group of poor, rugged boys from the slums into the church. Instead of being pleased, the minister was angry and Booth was told next time to bring them through the back door and seat them where they couldn't be seen. As he had feared, the Methodist Church of his day was becoming too "respectable."

His long hours in the pawnshop stretched out for six years; and though he often worked until 8 p.m., he would hurry to prayer meetings which would last until 10 p.m. Sometimes, after this, he would call on the sick and dying. It is said that he made hundreds of hospital calls before he was twenty years of age. He also did much street preaching late at night during these years. He soon became a leader in these enterprises; and at seventeen, he was made a local preacher by the Wesleyan Methodists.

Working with the outcast and poor of Nottingham brought increased burdens for the larger cities. Seeing London in 1849 at age twenty, he said, "What a city to save!" Sixteen years later he began to help save it.

Here in London he was without a friend and almost broke. For three years he worked as a clerk for a pawnbroker in the day, giving leisure time to working among the poor and did street preaching at night. A number of Methodist chapels opened to him for Sunday ministries, but his Superintendent discouraged him from entering the regular ministry. In 1851 a controversy arose in the Wesleyan Church over the question of lay representation, and a large number of ministers formed a group known as "Reformers." These Reformers offered Booth the pastorship of one of their chapels in London and a businessman offered to support him. He accepted and in 1852 went into full time preaching at a Methodist circuit in Spalding. Here he met Catherine Mumford, falling in love with her the third time he saw her on Good Friday, April 10. For two or three years he preached in various places with great success. Many souls were won.

Because the Reformers had an unsettled policy and organization, he and a number of others joined the "Methodist New Connexion" movement in 1854. His fame as a revivalist began to spread all over England. Hundreds professed conversion to Christ in almost every series of meetings held, while his sensational methods of preaching on the slum street corners often provoked disorder.

Catherine Mumford became his wife and an ideal co-worker on June 16, 1855, at Stockwell, New Chapel in South London. They were pressed into service immediately. As they arrived at the pier on the Island of Guernsey for their honeymoon, they found crowds of people begging them to conduct revival meetings there. The crowds were so large that the doors of the church had to be opened at 5:30 in order to allow the people to come in for the evening service. He was soon preaching in England's leading cities. . .London, Bristol, Bradford, Manchester, Sheffield and thousands professed faith in Christ. Once, in a space of a few months, Booth saw over 1,700 converts, an average of 23 per day. As the fourth month passed, the number rose past 2,000 and the Connexion leaders saw him as going too far too fast. His methods were "lusty American, not Victorian English," they said. How soon Wesley had been forgotten.

Their first child, William Bramwell, was born March 8, 1856. Six other children followed, all active in the work of the Army. They were Ballington (born July 28, 1859), Emma (born Jan. 8, 1860), Evangeline (born Dec. 25, 1865), Catherine, Herbert and Lucy, the youngest born in 1868.

In 1857 the Connexion cut short Booth's country-wide travels. He was given charge of one of their least-promising circuits, Brighouse, in Yorkshire. Yet pastoral work did not tie him down. He went to the local masses who needed him and initiated labor reforms and other worthwhile projects to help the residents. In 1858, the year that he became a fully ordained minister, he was given another circuit. . .Gateshead. Contrary to his own judgment, once more he obeyed and went; but his eyes strayed beyond the 1,000 strong congregation of Bethesda Chapel. It was the masses beyond the walls of the church that he was interested in.

The Methodist Church continually denied his request to be released from his regular circuit work as a pastor so that he could return to the field of evangelism again. Weary with the constant controversy, in July 1861 the Booths stepped out by faith, doing what they felt God had called them to do. He was 32 years old. About the same time, the Booths were both led into a Christian experience following John Wesley's views and teaching on sanctification, heart purity and holiness.

Now traveling in evangelism, he started in Cornwall, then on to Cardiff, Wales and Walsall. The crowds at Hayle, Cornwall, were too great to be accommodated in any building and great open-air meetings were held. The campaign stretched out to eighteen months. Fishermen rowed ten miles and villagers walked up to four miles to hear him preach. Booth claimed 7,000 Cornishmen became Christians. At Cardiff a tent was used. At Walsall in Staffordshire, he used many converts as testimonies of God's saving power. This 1863 visit drew 5,000 to the open-air preaching of Booth.

The beginnings of the great Salvation Army started July 2, 1865, as a large tent was erected on a Quaker burial ground in the Whitechapel neighborhood in East London. William Booth was now 36 years old. Another evangelist became ill and Booth substituted. Meetings were held every night for two weeks among the poor lower classes of the London slums. At midnight, upon returning home after a serious soul searching, he said, "I have found my destiny!" This was July 5, 1865. Converts streamed to the tent the next night. Soon they were using an unused warehouse.

The work was first called the East London (Christian) Revival Society, then the East London Christian Mission, and then the Christian Mission, firmly established by 1869. Open air meetings were held from 6 to 7 p.m. with an invitation to come to the evening meeting at the tent. These meetings continued on past the scheduled allotment; and, after rain, howling winds and a gang of ruffians had torn the tent down twice, they finally rented a large dance hall. Up to 600 would gather on Sunday following a night of dancing by citizens of another world the preceding night. Later he held evangelistic meetings at a wool warehouse and finally at an unused theater. Sometimes some would pour gunpowder in the room and create a blinding flash by setting fire to it. Frequently mud and stones were hurled through the windows, also.

Toiling on from this difficult beginning, a chain of missions was gradually formed with the power of God manifest in meeting after meeting. From now on Booth was to be found preaching wherever people would listen to him. . .dancing saloons, stables, sheds adjacent to pig sties, theater stages, circus rings, race course grandstands, footboards of railway carriages, ship-captain bridges and African huts! But he was foremost a specialist in open-air services and street corners. People were often stricken down in his meetings, overwhelmed with a sense of the presence and power of God.

Opposition came. . .it was not uncommon to see Salvationists end up with broken ankles and wrists. One had a piece of flesh bitten out of his arm. . .another, alone on inspection tour, was pelted and mobbed for one and a half hours. Another had lime thrown into the eyes of his child. One woman convert was kicked in the womb and left to die. The first march General and Mrs. Booth made to Albert Hall in Sheffield ended up in a riot. They, their officers and soldiers arrived at the meeting wounded, bleeding and battered. Their clothes were torn and covered with filth, their band instruments smashed. This was not to be uncommon. Often every available hall or room would be denied them. Both once wrote from Salisbury, "The evangelists have to get off the street and into houses to escape this mob. Police refuse protection. Nevertheless, there is a good society. A lot are saved. We must not give up! We will not!" Many times in his life he would be stoned, battered, shoved, cursed and almost killed. In 1889, at least 669 Salvation Army members were assaulted, including 251 women. Some were killed and many were maimed. A "Skelton Army" of ruffians devoted themselves to disrupting Salvation Army meetings. They frequently stormed the meeting halls by the hundreds (on one occasion, 4,000) broke out windows and wrecked the inside of the buildings. Fifty buildings were wrecked. The police did little to assist Booth. Once, while defending themselves, 86 Army members were arrested and imprisoned on disorderly conduct charges. Booth had his own private bodyguard, Peter Monk, an Irish prize fighter and one of his converts. By 1872 he was running five "Food-for-the-Mission Shops," selling cheap meals.

This militant evangelism culminated in the adoption of the title "Salvation Army" and the reorganization of the movement along the quasi-military lines of a well disciplined army on August 7, 1878. Booth had been distressed at the lack of direction, and with this new set up, could really assert himself as the leader. The name developed from an incident in May 1878. Booth was dictating a letter to his secretary, George Scott Railton (his faithful associate for 48 years), and said, "We are a volunteer army." Bramwell, his son, heard his father and said, "Volunteer, I'm no volunteer, I'm a regular!" Railton was instructed to cross out the word volunteer and substitute the word *salvation*. Soon they were tagged, "Soap, Soup and Salvation Army."

The new, almost dictatorial leadership of Booth was dynamic. By January 1879 he had 81 stations, 127 full time evangelists (100 of his converts), and 75,000 services a year going. In 1880 it expanded to the United States and adopted uniforms. The same year the first band was formed in Salisbury. A new headquarters was opened in London in 1881 as well as the work in France. In 1882 India was sent workers.

Its orders and regulations were patterned after those of the British Army. All workers assumed military titles, its trainees became "cadets," local units were designated as "Corps," places of worship became known as "Citadels" or "Outposts," and their evangelistic undertakings were called "Campaigns." The converts were organized into a carefully disciplined group. Of course, the uniforms, officers, organization, regulations and discipline, plus the title "General" for Booth attracted derision and criticism at first. Nevertheless, the "Army" was reaching people ignored by more staid church bodies! He launched a successful crusade against white slavery in 1885.

A whirlwind eleven week campaign was conducted in 1886 with Booth preaching from New York to Kansas City. Town after town listened spellbound as he thundered at the crowds, his long body swaying back and forth on the platform, his hair and flowing beard rumpled, his arms clasped behind his back. He spoke for 200 hours and was heard by 180,000 people. He pulled together the U.S. organization that had fragmented into three parts.

Back home in London, the sight of homeless men leaning on the rails of London Bridge prompted the beginning of heavy social work. Now the image of the Army suddenly changed as in 1887 the social service programs began to expand as General Booth fought poverty with practical philanthropy. He realized that the physical and social environment of the masses made it difficult for them to appreciate the message of the Army. He accordingly embarked upon social work to clear the way for evangelism. These services ranged from night shelters and free breakfasts to the selection and training of prospective immigrants and their settlement overseas.

Booth's best selling *Darkest England and the Way Out* was published in 1890, showing victorian England how to deal with poverty and vice plus the need of religious and social redemption. He proposed the concentration of the nation's philanthropic funds upon the slums, hitherto largely left to the care of the local parish churches, and suggested a list of practical expedients to this end such as advocating the reclamation of unemployable persons in farm colonies.

No small credit for gain in prestige is due General Booth's wife. Catherine was a woman of charm and ability, winning the sympathy of many of the upper classes for the new movement. When she was 59, it was discovered she had cancer. General Booth had already accepted meetings in Holland, and upon hearing the news, was about to cancel. She insisted that he go. "I'm ready to die, but many of those people over there are not." He did go for an abbreviated visit; and upon his return, he found her very weak. She died October 4, 1890. The streets of London were crowded for four miles as the funeral procession went by! More than 10,000 people went to the cemetery. Added to his sorrow was the death of General Booth's daughter Emma in a railroad accident.

At the time of Catherine's death (after 25 years of ministry together in the work of the Army), the Salvation Army had 2,900 centers in 34 countries and was receiving 600 telegrams and 5,400 letters a week.

Another trip to America was made in 1895, and Booth found over 500 people engaged in the work of the Army. He held 340 meetings in 86 cities, speaking to 437,000 people resulting in 2,200 converts. In 24 weeks he spent 847 hours on a train. Twice, while in America, he opened the Senate in prayer. He talked to President McKinley for twenty minutes on one of his tours.

General Booth was now being praised by such diverse men as Charles Spurgeon, Winston Churchill and Cardinal Manning. The Prince of Wales became a most ardent patron; and upon his coronation as Edward VII in 1902, Booth was officially invited to the festivities. On June 24, 1904, in a visit to Buckingham Palace, the King asked the General what his recreations were. Booth, writing in his autograph album, replied, "Sir, some men have a passion for art, fame and gold. I have a passion for souls."

Many found him dictatorial and hard to work with. Members of his own family denounced him as their leader and founded separate organizations. Gypsy Smith had left him because of his rigidity and D. L. Moody would not support him because he felt there was a threat to the local church. But no one could deny his compassion.

He was constantly telling his family, his soldiers, all England, to go and do something. He could not rest. . .once writing, "I am very tired, but must go on. . .on. . .I cannot stand still. I have worked today and laid down again when I could sit no longer and then got up to go on again. A fire is in my bones. . ." Once in South Africa, he talked for seven hours, his heart so yearning over the lost. Souls possessed him day and night, well or ill. Once his son found the old warrior pacing up and down the floor late at night. "What are you thinking about?" asked the son. "Ah, Bramwell, I'm thinking about the people's sin. What will people do with their sin?" When Booth denounced sin, people sat spellbound. They wept, hung their heads with conviction, their bosoms heaving with emotion. Conviction and conversion usually followed. As many as 3,000 at one time were known to have been moved to tears. Once in an outburst of concern for the lost, he exclaimed, "Oh, God, what can I say? Souls! Souls! Souls! My heart hungers for souls!"

Passing from one side of Great Britain to the other, General Booth made a 29 day, 1,224 mile motor tour in 1904, holding 164 meetings, gathering crowds from day to day. He visited the United States one more time in 1907. His farewell message was given on the steps of New York City Hall to 2,500 people. The year 1908 found him in Scandinavia; 1910 in Switzerland, Holland, Germany, Italy and Denmark. On May 9, 1912, he gave his last major speech to 7,000 Salvationists at London's Albert Hall.

As his aged eyes became weak, an unsuccessful operation was performed on May 23rd. Two days later it was found that he had an infection and that he would lose his sight completely. Upon going blind, he said, "God knows best. I have done what I could for God and the people with my eyes. Now I must do what I can for God and the people without my eyes."

When asked for the secret of his success, William Booth said:

> I will tell you the secret, God has had all there was of me. There have been men with greater brains than I, men with greater opportunities. But from the day I got the poor of London on my heart and caught a vision of all Jesus Christ

could do with them, on that day I made up my mind that God would have all of William Booth there was. And if there is anything of power in the Salvation Army today, it is because God has had all the adoration of my heart, all the power of my will and all the influence of my life.

As he died, he turned to his son Bramwell and said, "I'm leaving you a bonnie handful." As his body lay in state, 65,000 to 150,000 marched by to pay tribute to the man who not only talked, but did something for the masses. The funeral was held at a vast exhibition hall on Hammersmith Road drawing 40,000 including Queen Mary, who sat next to an ex-prostitute, a convert of General Booth's. Traffic in London stopped for two hours as his funeral procession of 10,000 marching Salvationists went through the downtown streets.

He was succeeded by his son Bramwell Booth. Eventually his daughter Evangeline became the Commander-in-Chief.

It is estimated Booth traveled five million miles and preached 60,000 sermons in his 60 years of ministry. This included five trips to the United States and Canada, three to Australia and South Africa, two to India, one to Japan and several to the various European countries. Sixteen thousand officers were serving in his Army.

Booth was the author of many favorite revival hymns and several books, such as *Salvation Soldiers* (1890) and *Religion For Every Day* (1902). Some of his works have gone into twenty languages. He started *War Cry*, the official organ of The Army, on December 26, 1879, with 17,000 copies.

The Life
And Ministry Of

David Brainerd
1718 -1747

DAVID BRAINERD

BORN: April 20, 1718   **DIED:** October 9, 1747

Haddam, Conn.   Northampton, Mass.

LIFE SPAN: 19 years, 5 months, 19 days

He was only 29 when he died. . .his gravestone simply says, "A faithful and laborious missionary to the Stockbridge, Delaware and Susquehanna tribes of Indians." But in truth David Brainerd's life sacrifice reached out and touched the whole world, challenging more people into Christian service than perhaps any other man that ever lived. The mere mention of the name, Brainerd, automatically triggers the mind to think of dedication in a way that perhaps has never been equaled. He would travel 15,000 miles on horseback. One small compelling book - *David Brainerd's Journal*, which he kept from June 19, 1745, to June 19, 1746, plus his diaries of his days before and after this time, are still used of God today to inspire and convict the Christian world in the matter of Christian service.

David was the sixth of nine children born into the home of Hezekiah and Dorothy (Mason) Brainerd. Details of his childhood are scanty, but he grew up in a country house just above the west bank of the Connecticut River, two miles outside of Haddam. His father was a country squire, a local justice of the peace, and a Christian, as was his mother. His father died when he was nine; and the death of his mother in March 1732 brought additional great grief to 14 year old David, who was by then seeking to find what conversion was all about. From ages 15 to 19 he lived with his sister Jerusha, who had just married Samuel Spencer. In April 1738 he returned to Haddam to live and to study with the pastor of his youth, Phineas Fiske. Brainerd soon became a serious student of the Bible and ignored the other pleasures in which most young people were participating. Fiske died in the fall and Brainerd, like Luther, continued desperately seeking peace with God. By February 1739 he was setting aside whole days of secret fasting and almost incessant prayer as he strove for acceptance with God.

Finally on July 12, 1739, as he returned to his secret place of prayer, God spoke to him as light dawned and he had a glorious salvation experience. Now he wondered why all the world could not see "this lovely, blessed, and excellent way." He states as he was walking in a dark thick grove, unspeakable glory seemed to open to the view and apprehension of his soul. He was then 21 years of age.

In September 1739 David entered Yale University. It was a terribly cold winter and a bout with the measles laid him aside that first year. Trying to catch up only caused greater maladies; and by August 1740, he was weak and spitting up blood. Consumption or tuberculosis of the lungs was the plague of colonial New England. He returned to Yale on about November 6, 1740, to see a marked spiritual change in the school. George Whitefield had visited Yale on October 27, and it seemed a pentecostal flame had hit the school. Gil Tennent of New Jersey had also preached with great power in March 1740 in New Haven. Brainerd and two other students were soon distinguished for their zeal and visited many other students "for conversation and prayer." On April 19, Ebenezer Pemberton visited Yale and gave a stirring address about missionary work to the Indians. The next day, on his 23rd birthday, Brainerd vowed "to be wholly the Lord's, to be forever devoted to his service."

The Great Awakening was now at its peak; and despite Jonathan Edwards' efforts to keep everything in decency and order, things got out of hand. Tennent had preached his impassioned sermon, *The Danger of an Unconverted Ministry,* simply reinforcing Whitefield's sentiments. People began to turn against their ministers and hold "separate" meetings.

So as a result, as Brainerd entered his third year at Yale in the fall of 1741, a rule was made, "Voted, that if any student of this College shall directly or indirectly say, that the Rector, either of the Trustees or Tutors are hypocrites, carnal or unconverted men, he shall for the first offense make a public confession in the Hall, and for the second offense be expelled." Soon in a private conversation, when asked what he thought about a certain tutor, David replied, "He has no more grace than this chair." This charge was harsh, and based only on one prayer of the leader, which David called, "unusually pathetical." Actually, the man was quite spiritual. A freshman overheard and reported the conversation. When Brainerd refused to publicly confess this, which he felt was a private matter, he was expelled in February 1742. Afterwards, he sought forgiveness, wrote out a full and complete confession, and had others intercede for him. . .but to no avail. The authorities would not re-instate him.

On April 20 (24th birthday) Brainerd wrote, ". . .I hardly ever so longed to live to God and to be altogether devoted to him; I wanted to wear out my life in his service and for his glory. . ." He waged a constant fight against the bitterness of his disappointment over his expulsion from Yale. In June he began to spend some days in fasting and prayer. He was at a loss as to what the Lord wanted him to do. On July 29, 1742, he was licensed to preach as a Presbyterian at Danbury, Connecticut. He spent the summer with another young bachelor friend--Joseph Bellamy. They worshipped and preached in a barn which served as a meeting house for Bellamy's small congregation in Woodbury, Connecticut. Brainerd's first sermon was on July 30 at Southbury, Connecticut, using I Peter 4:8 as his text; and his first message to the Indians was soon after, on August 12, near the Connecticut-New York border. He traveled as an itinerant preacher for several months. In September 1742 he had to leave New Haven quickly for unlawful preaching.

On November 19 he received a summons from Pemberton of New York City to come and discuss the question of ministry to the Indians in those parts. On November 25 he met with the commissioners of the Scotch Society. As part of his examination, he delivered a sermon, most probably in Pemberton's church. He was grieved for the congregation, "that they should sit there to hear such a dead dog as I preach." He felt he was totally unworthy to preach to others so much better than himself.

He preached from place to place in the winter, including a farewell sermon to his family and friends in a home in East Haddam on February 1, 1743. He then served as a supply preacher at East Hampton, Long Island, New York, for six weeks. On his last Sunday there, March 13, although he could hardly stand up, he preached for an hour and a half. The congregation pressed him to stay permanently. But the next day he left for work among the Indians. He said later, "I never, since I began to preach, could feel any freedom to enter into other men's labours and settle down in the ministry where the gospel was preached before." He felt he had to preach where Christ was not named nor known. He left for his life's work March 25, 1743.

He was assigned to Stockbridge, Massachusetts, and arrived there March 31, 1743, and began his ministry the next day. He was stationed 20 miles west between Stockbridge and the Hudson River at a place called Kaunaumeek, 18 miles southeast of Albany. Without conversation or company, he was very lonely even though the Indians were cordial to him. On April 20, (25th birthday) he spent the day fasting alone in the woods in prayer. His diet was hasty-pudding, boiled corn, and bread baked in ashes. His lodging was a heap of straw, laid upon boards in a log room without any floor. He traveled one and one half miles each way daily on foot in order to see the Indians. A Stockbridge Christian became his interpreter and friend. Brainerd learned to pray with the Indians in their language. They translated Psalms and hymns and started an "English" school. By the first of August he had completed building his hut and had a better place to sleep. But other problems mounted. He had to go or send ten or more miles for bread to eat and it would turn moldy and sour before he could eat all of it. The presence and worldly conversation of some irreligious Dutchmen oppressed him more than all the difficulties of his wilderness life. He made four brief trips to New York during this time, his last one including a stop at New Haven to observe the commencement exercises of September 14, 1743, in which he should have been included. One final attempt to have him re-instated with Jonathan Edwards and Aaron Burr interceding was to no avail. Stopping at Bellamy's, he became seriously ill. Recovering sufficiently he returned to his station, Kaunaumeek, on October 4.

One the day after Christmas he wrote, "was very much fatigued with my journey, wherein I underwent great hardships; was very much exposed and very wet by falling in a river." The ordination of a friend, Samuel Hopkins, that week left him depressed as he could not understand the accompanying levity, celebration and food. In January 1744 he spent the middle of the winter alone in his little hut, yet they were happy hours. On Sunday, March 11, he preached his last sermon at Kaunaumeek, as he was now seeking new tribes to win to Christ.

He again received a call to East Hampton to be the pastor. Suffering weakness and headache, he died inwardly to two attractive calls, writing, "Resolved to go on still with the Indian affair, if divine providence permitted; although I had before felt some inclination to go to East Hampton." His other call to Millington was likewise turned down.

The commissioners instructed him to go to Pennsylvania. He again had a serious sick spell for three days and went home to Haddam for the first time in 15 months. Now 26 years of age, he left home again. He left Kaunaumeek

April 30.

Spending some days at Salisbury, Connecticut, he left May 7, arriving on May 13 at Easton, Pennsylvania, within the forks of the Delaware River.

Brainerd was well received by the Indians and usually taught them in the chief's house. Traveling some 70 miles back to New York, Brainerd was ordained on June 11, 1744, by the Presbytery of New York. On June 19 he left friends and benefactors to seek again God's chosen ones in the remote wilderness.

By the end of the summer some 40 Indians were listening to his message. He was plagued with pain and had difficulty controlling his legs after long hours on horseback. He also had to cope with Tattamy, his interpreter, who was totally unfamiliar with the white man's Bible. In July a flicker of heart interest by the Indians caused him to work hard preaching and translating. One time he was asking the Lord to take him home. Then he heard the Indians intended to have an idolatrous feast and dance. Desire to live surged back into him as he used his only weapon--prayer--and the Indians changed their plans.

During this time he lived much of the time with the Hunter family at a place known as Hunter's Settlement. Brainerd was the supply minister to the whites there along with his ministry to the Indians. The rest of the summer he lied in "illness and uselessness." The first week of August he preached to the Indians twice, although "obligated to sit down the whole time." By September he was somewhat recovered and took a three week vacation. It was a journey of recuperation and pleasure, of visiting home and friends back in New England.

He now had a desire to go westward to reach the Indians on the Susquehanna River. Brainerd, an associate Eliab Bryam, Tattamy and two other Indians left on October 2. His horse fell down and broke her leg, so Brainerd killed her and continued to the nearest house 30 miles away on foot. The picture of the two young ministers alternately riding their one horse must have been intriguing. They were well received by the Indians, spent a few days there, and then returned the 70 miles where a new horse was given to Brainerd on October 12.

Resuming his life, sick and lonely, alternately cheerful and dejected, he began to build a house for himself with the help of others. Moving into his new quarters, he spent December 6 in prayer and fasting "to implore the blessing of God on myself, on my poor people, on my friends, and on the church God." Beginning at Christmas he went through a terrible month of despondency. Things brightened up on Sunday, February 17, 1745, when he preached to a group of white people coming from scattered frontier homes to have Communion. He greatly appreciated his friends, both white and Indian; and on March 7, he left them for a few weeks' trip to New England. In March and April he rode more than 600 miles searching New Jersey, New York and Connecticut to find a companion and the support for the same. This goal was not realized, for none was "qualified or disposed for this good work." So he returned alone to the Forks of the Delaware to continue his work. On April 20 (27th birthday) he was at the Abington Presbyterian Church between

Philadelphia and Neshaminy for a three-day ministry.

Weak in body, Brainerd and Tattamy left May 8 for their first major trip to the interior Indians along the Susquehanna River. By passing the original contact they had made the previous October, they reached Shamokin, the headquarters for several tribes of Indians, stopped off at other settlements and returned home, the round trip taking 22 days. The 340 mile journey left Brainerd weak and dejected, depressed and disillusioned about the prospects among the Indians in that area. Except for Tattamy and his wife, who both were growing spiritually, he considered his past year almost a failure. He returned May 30.

He then heard about a group of Indians at a place called Crossweeksung (9 miles southeast of Trenton) in New Jersey, about 80 miles southeast of the Forks of Delaware. He arrived June 19, 1745. He spent two weeks there with a good deal of conviction, tears and interest amongst the Indians. Upon his return to the Forks, these Indians also seemed to be much more responsive to his ministry. On July 21 he baptized Tattamy and his wife, his first converts among the Indians. He went back to Crossweeksung and experienced the most glorious week in his life. On August 8 the power of God came down on his little group of 65 as he preached. The sudden and unexpected seizure of the Indians was followed by earnest prayers. Many genuine conversions took place. News traveled and soon other Indians were coming to hear the young white preacher. Members of the careless white community began to show up also and get converted. On August 25 he baptized 25 of the Indians and the years of prayer and suffering were beginning to bear some fruit.

He decided to make one last effort to evangelize the Indians along the Susquehanna River and spent the month of September (9-28) attempting this but with no apparent success. Back at Crossweeksung on October 5, he was overjoyed at the difference to the response of the Gospel. Others were saved and baptized. Christmas had a new meaning to both preacher and hearer; and after two years of barrenness, Brainerd rejoiced greatly as he reaped some spiritual fruit.

On January 31, 1746, another milestone was reached--Brainerd engaged a schoolmaster for the Indians and a dozen primers were passed out. In February he visited his "parish" back at the Forks being "under great weakness and some pain." Some evangelists (Indian converts) from Crossweeksung went with him. He encouraged some of his former friends at the Fork to move to Crossweeksung. Back at this site he had a very ill week in mid-March. He encouraged the Indians to develop spring planting at a settlement at Cranberry, 15 miles distant, which they did. His attempt to colonize the converts as farmers was not successful. There were now about 150 who followed him and his directions. On April 20 (28th birthday) he preached the Easter story from Luke 24 to the Indians. On April 27 another milestone was reached--the Indians took the Lord's Supper. He settled down at Cranberry on May 3 and a place of worship was established known as Bethel. He was tempted to stay here. However, back in his heart were the pagan Indians of the Susquehanna River area where he had already failed three times to make any headway.

Finally on August 12, he left his friends at Cranberry and with six Indian evangelists attempted his fourth trip to the Susquehanna River area. He had never gone further west than Shamokin before, but now he desired to go an additional 100 miles to a site near present day Lockhaven, Pennsylvania. He recorded such things as ". . .sweat much in the night, so that my linen was almost wringing wet all night, was exceedingly weak, so that I could scarcely ride; it seemed sometimes as if I must fall off from my horse, and lie in the open woods. . ."

This trip finally broke his health completely and he had to curtail much of it. Many might ask, "why did he go on this journey despite his great weakness and ill health?" He simply could not confine himself to one spot, when so many men were dying without Christ everywhere. Back at Shamokin on September 6 he clung to his life, "coughing and spitting blood." On September 20 he arrived back at Cranberry. Brainerd now realized that the tuberculosis of his lungs was going to destroy his body. He felt somewhat guilty in that he had recklessly injured his health and aggravated his illness. But in reality, his zeal and outdoor life probably prolonged his days since his problem had started several years prior while at Yale. On October 6 he had his last blessed day at Cranberry, having the Lord's Supper with 40 converts and baptizing two adults. His final harvest was now 85 Indians. November 3 was his last day as pastor of his flock in Cranberry. He spent the long winter in Elizabethtown, New Jersey, with Jonathan Dickinson. Rallying in health he made one last visit to his Indian converts on March 18-20, 1747, and bid them goodbye for the last time. On April 20 (29th birthday) he spent the day mostly in bed at the Dickinsons. He left for New England the next day, not realizing that his 59 year old host would pass on two days before Brainerd. Brainerd was invited to Jonathan Edwards' house, by probably both the preacher and his 17 year daughter, Jerusha, whom Brainerd had greatly admired even as a young teenage girl. He visited his kin-folk at Haddam, (May 1) bidding farewell to his favorite sister, Jerusha Spencer, little realizing that he would get news of her death in two more months. Arriving at the Edwards' home on May 28, he was vastly better and cheerful. David's petition in family prayer was usually "that we might not outlive our usefulness." Jerusha was his nurse for 19 weeks, devoting herself with great delight because she looked on him as an eminent servant of Jesus Christ. He wrote letters signing them, "your dying brother." He took his last horseback ride and prayed with the family for the last time on August 11. A room on the first floor was set aside for him the following week as he could not climb steps. He went to church for the last time September 2. Edwards described his last days--swollen feet, constant pain, discharge of purulent matter, broken whispers, agonies of body. His last Sunday, October 4, he recorded this touching conversation with Jerusha in appreciation of her constant companionship and love.

> "Dear Jerusha. . .though, if I thought I should not see you, and be happy with you in another world, I could not bear to part with you. But we shall spend a happy eternity together."

On Wednesday he discussed his Indian work with his brother John, who succeeded him at Bethel; and on Friday, October 9, it was all over. His last words were "He will come, and will not tarry. I shall soon be in glory; soon be with God and His angels." He was buried on Monday with Jonathan Edwards conducting the funeral. Four months later a grieving Jerusha, in her 18th year, took sick; and in five days, on February 14, 1748, joined David in heaven and was buried next to him.

John Wesley said, "Let every preacher read carefully over the life of David Brainerd" and distributed his life story to all his societies. F. W. Robertson, Ion Keith Falconer, Robert Murray McCheyne, A. J. Gordon, Francis Ashbury, Jim Elliott, Thomas Coke, William Carey and Henry Martyn all were motivated to service through Brainerd, amongst others.

The Life
And Ministry Of

Peter Cartwright
1785- 1872

PETER CARTWRIGHT

BORN: September 1, 1785   **DIED:** September 25, 1872
Amherst County, Virginia   **Pleasant Plains, Illinois**
LIFE SPAN: 87 years, 24 days

Cartwright traveled for nearly 70 years preaching the gospel throughout the midwest with the frontier preacher's typical three books in his saddlebags: a Bible, a hymn book, and the book of Methodist Discipline. Cartwright stands unsurpassed as America's backwoods camp meting preacher. His spiritual power, native wit, and ability to handle ruffians who would seek to break up his meetings made him famous around the world.

His calling was to evangelize pioneer America in its westward march toward the Mississippi River. Tens of thousands accepted Christ as their Saviour, who otherwise would have never heard of Him. His "hellfire and brimstone" preaching matched his character and personality. He was opposed to easy religion, education and culture in the ministry.

It is only fair to say that Cartwright did object to the excesses of some of the camp meetings, labeling such things as the "jerks," the "barks," the "running," and the "trances," as works of the devil. His 70 years of traveling were in Kentucky, Tennessee, Ohio, Indiana and Illinois where he spent his last 48 years.

He was born of poor parents, the Justinian Cartwright's. His father served as a Revolutionary soldier in the war of the American Revolution. He was an unbeliever but the mother was Methodist. In 1790, shortly after the colonies gained their independence, the family moved to Kentucky. The wilderness through which they passed was filled with hostile Indians, so 200 families banded together with 100 well armed young men used as guards as they traveled. They first settled at Lancaster.

In the fall of 1793 the family moved to the southern part of the state, settling in Logan County, nine miles south of Russellville, and within one mile of the state of Tennessee. With father's consent, John Lurton, a traveling preacher, was invited to preach in the Cartwright's cabin. A Methodist church was located several miles from their home in a general region known as Rogue's Harbor. Here refugees from almost all parts of the Union, who had fled from the scenes of their law-breaking to escape punishment, were gathered. Sunday was set apart for hunting, fishing, horse racing, card playing and dancing. It was in such an atmosphere that Cartwright grew up.

Cartwright enjoyed every sin possible. His father did not restrain him and gave him a race horse and a pack of cards. As civilization advanced, churches sprang up, a school was opened and Peter went in for book learning for a short while, during which time he learned to read, write, and cipher.

In 1800 and 1801 an amazing series of meetings took place at Cane Ridge. Some 1,000 to 2,000 were converted including Cartwright. As many as seven preachers would be preaching at once to various groups.

Specifically his conversion was as follows: In late 1800 (age 15) he attended a wedding that had the usual dancing and drinking. Once home, he became convicted of sin and fell on his knees, asking God to have mercy upon him. His mother sprang from her bed, dropped to her knees and prayed for her son. Cartwright promised the Lord if he would be spared, he would seek and serve Him. he returned his horses, gave away his cards, fasted, watched and prayed, still not saved.

In the spring of 1801 the local Presbyterian church was having an awakening and overflowed its facilities, so they met in a shady grove at a place called Cane Ridge.   At this camp meeting many were saved and Christians shouted for joy. On Saturday night, Cartwright heard as if it were a voice from Heaven saying, "Thy sins are all forgiven thee." Divine light flashed all around him and unspeakable joy sprang up in his soul. It was the night of his conversion and lasted all night. This was in May 1801. In June he joined the Methodist Church, which he served the rest of his life. He soon began to speak and exhort in local meetings.

From this time, because of the impact of the Kentucky revivals, a religious revival movement prevailed through almost all the inhabited parts of the western country.   The Methodist camp -meeting had now been established. Cartwright soon became known as "The Kentucky Boy." later the "Backwoods Preacher." His only theological training appears to have been derived from the diligent study of his Bible and habitual prayer, along with experiences derived from his continuous labors in religious gatherings. He began to convert the lads of the neighborhood with much success.

In May 1802 he received a certificate from the preacher-in-charge that he was permitted to exercise his gifts as an exhorter in the Methodist Episcopal Church, "so long as his practices were agreeable to the gospel." This was a license to preach the Gospel, and he was only 16 years old. His salary as a single man was supposed to be $80 a year. In the fall of 1802 the family moved into Lewiston County.

This new territory was 80 miles away from any regular circuit. When he applied to the presiding elder for letters of recommendation to the local Methodist Episcopal Church in the new region, he found that the paper which he had received authorized him to hold meetings and organize classes throughout all the region he was traveling. In essence, he was to organize a new Methodist Circuit. He felt the need for education and went to a place called Brown's Academy for a time. He soon collected a small class from scattered Methodists that were around, had a few conversions and doors began to open. School lasted several months but that was about all. In the fall of 1803 he reported his successes and the plan of the circuit, which was made up of scattered members, now organized into classes. It was called the Livingston Circuit. On October 10, 1803, having just turned 18, he threw himself into the ranks of circuit riding preachers, traveling through the large Red River Circuit of Kentucky an then later the Waynesville Circuit which covered a part of Tennessee.

Although Cartwright did on baptismal occasions immerse, he sprinkled for the most part. He had a running conflict with the Baptists from place to place whose preachers would rush in and try to take his converts off into the water. On one occasion Baptist preachers substituted for him. Cartwright was convinced that sprinkling was sufficient baptism; and when the local Baptists requested that his converts be dipped, he requested that he, being their spiritual father, ought to be allowed to join their church as much as the new converts. He testified of his baptism, which was not immersion; and upon their refusal of him to become a member, all his converts decided to also follow Cartwright's leadership, so a Methodist Church was started on the spot.

At the conference held in October 1804, he was sent as the junior preacher to the Salt River and Shelbyville Circuits, which extended into Indiana. People dressed plainly, attended meetings faithfully, wore no jewelry or ruffles, and would frequently walk three or four miles to class meetings on Sunday.

In 1805-06 he was on the Scioto (Ohio) circuit. It was during these days that a genuine attempt was made to break up one of his Sunday morning meetings. Two men deliberately tried to lead in a disruption of a meeting. Cartwright ordered the magistrate, who was drunk, to take the disturbers into custody. This was refused, and Cartwright himself went into the audience and knocked both men and the magistrate to the ground. Soon law officials came to the rescue; and before it was all over, 30 were taken as prisoners. Things were confused until the evening meeting which he described:

> My text was, "The gates of hell shall not prevail." In about thirty minutes the power of God fell on the congregation in such a manner as is seldom seen; the people fell in every direction right and left, front and rear. It was supposed that not less than three hundred fell like dead men in mighty battle; and there was no need of calling mourners, for they were strewn all over the campground; loud wailings went up to Heaven from sinners for mercy, and a general shout from Christians, so that the noise was heard afar off. Our meeting lasted all night, and Monday and Monday night; and when we closed on Tuesday, there were two hundred who had professed religion and about that number joined the church.

On August 18, 1808, he married Frances Gaines, on her 19th birthday. The Cartwrights were to have 9 children, seven daughters and two sons. The 1808 Conference was held at Liberty Hill, Tennessee, on October 13. A week prior, October 4, he was ordained an elder by Bishop McKendree. McKendree instructed him in English grammar and laid out for him a course of study and reading, which the young disciple faithfully pursued. This was the year he lost his father, and had to take some time off to take care of arrangements at the homestead. In 1809 he attended the conference at Cincinnati, where he was appointed to the Livingston Circuit. This is where he began six years before. Active members numbered 427 in that area. The whole Western Conference (basically Tennessee and Ohio) jumped from 9,000 members in 1804, when Cartwright joined the conference, to 30,741 members in 1811. He was made presiding elder in the fall of 1812 by Bishop Asbury, at the Fountain Head, Tennessee, Conference held November 1, a position he held for 60 years. In the fall of 1815 he was elected delegate to the second general conference of the Methodist Church in America, to be held at Baltimore, Maryland, in 1816. From that time on he was always present (12 times) at the quadrennial gatherings of the denomination in the United States, except for one time (1832) when sickness in the family prevented it. For the local annual conferences which we have been describing, he went 50 consecutive years, except for one session, when a kindred reason eliminated his presence. Circuit riding and preaching at stated quarterly meetings and camp meetings filled his life. He was not afraid of bishops and often thundered at them, to their faces, at General Conferences. Each six weeks he made the rounds of his circuit and conference, visiting each church, preaching, holding revivals, presiding at business meetings, and seeing hundreds of souls converted.

The 1818 conference in Nashville, Tennessee, had an often-repeated story transpire. On Monday night in early October, Cartwright was speaking at a Presbyterian Church and had just repeated his text, Mark 8:36, when in walked General Stonewall Jackson. The host preacher pulled Cartwright's coat and whispered loud, "General Jackson has come in; General Jackson has come in." Cartwright felt indignation running all over him and looking at the audience said audibly, "Who is General Jackson? If he doesn't get his soul converted, God will damn him as quick as he would a Guinea negro." The congregation, General Jackson and all smiled and laughed out loud. The host preacher went to the hotel early the next morning to apologize for Cartwright's conduct. A little later Cartwright passed by the hotel and met the General on the pavement. Jackson reached out his hand and said:

> "Mr. Cartwright, you are a man after my own heart. I am very much surprised at Mr. Mac, to think he would suppose that I would be offended at you. No sir, I told him that I highly approved of your independence; that a minister of Jesus Christ ought to love everybody and fear no mortal man. I told Mr. Mac that if I had a few thousand such independent, fearless officers as you were and a well-drilled army, I could take old England."

In June 1820 another Cartwright incident took place. On the return home from the Baltimore General Conference, the 1,000 mile journey on horseback was fatiguing. Riding up to a tavern in Knoxville, Tennessee, for the purpose of dining, he an Brother Walker found it loaded with drunks, so they went to another tavern. Again the same reception, hence they again agreed not to stop. Finally they came to a house with a sign over the door, "Private Entertainment and New Cider." They were refreshed, but the cider was more than they anticipated it would be; and they rode on to the next stop more drunk than sober. Cartwright bade Brother Walker goodbye and journeyed on toward his home in Christian County, Kentucky. Saturday night came and found him in a strange region of the country and in the hills, knobs and spurs of the Cumberland Mountains. Cartwright desired to spend Sunday with God's people, but there was nothing but scattered population and no Gospel center. Weekends simply meant to hunt, drink, visit or dance. In the evening he hailed a decent house and asked the landlord for quarters. The host agreed he could stay but said a party that night with a dance would keep him awake. The next such lodge was seven miles distant, so Cartwright decided to stay here. He took his seat in one corner of the house as the dance commenced in the main room. He finally settled in his mind that he would spend the next day there seeking to preach to the group. Suddenly a beautiful, ruddy, young lady walked gracefully up to him, dropped a handsome curtsy and with winning smiles, invited him out to take a dance with her. Cartwright resolved to try a desperate experiment. He rose as gracefully as he could with many emotions. The young lady moved to his right side, whereupon Cartwright grasped her right hand with his. They walked on the floor with the whole company pleased at this act of politeness by the young lady. The colored fiddler began to tune up. Cartwright asked the fiddler to hold a moment and stated for several years he had not undertaken any matter of importance without first asking the blessing of God upon it, and further stated that he now desired to ask the blessing of God upon the beautiful young lady and the whole company, seeing that they had shown such politeness to a total stranger.

He continued, "Let's all kneel down and pray," and instantly he dropped to his knees and began to pray with all the power of soul and body that he could command. The young lady tried to get loose from him, but he held her hand tight. Presently she feel on her knees. Some of the crowd knelt, some stood, some fled, some sat still--all looked curious. The fiddler ran off into the kitchen mumbling. While Cartwright prayed, some wept, and wept aloud, and some cried for mercy. He arose from his knees and commenced an exhortation, then sang a hymn. The young lady lay prostrate, crying earnestly for mercy. Cartwright exhorted again, sang, and prayed nearly all night. About 15 were converted. The meeting lasted all day Sunday, and another 15 were converted on the Lord's day. Cartwright organized a society, voted 32 into the church, and sent them a preacher. This was the beginning of a great and glorious revival in the region and several of the young men converted at this dance became useful ministers.

Determining to move from Kentucky in 1823 to Illinois (age 38) he set out to explore the state of Illinois, and on November 15, 1824, reached Pleasant Plains with his family. This would now become his home for the rest of his life. His reasons for moving were:

First, I would get rid of the evil of slavery. Second, I could raise my children where work was not thought a degradation. Third, I believed I could better my temporal circumstances, and procure lands for my children as they grow up. Fourth, I could carry the Gospel to destitute souls.

The grip was not without tragedy for a freak accident killed one of his daughters en route. In October, as his family slept outside on their trip, a tree that had rotted away fell on their third daughter as they slept, killing her outright.

Cartwright was transferred to the Illinois Conference and appointed to travel to Sangamon (Ill.) circuit. He was presiding elder here for 45 years and attended 16 annual meetings of the Illinois Conference. He stayed with various circuits in the state for the remainder of his life.

In 1833 Cartwright ran for Illinois legislature and had the distinction of beating Abraham Lincoln for the position. He was chosen a second time for the same position. In 1842 he built a little church in Pleasant Plains, so that his family would have a local place to worship. This was the same year that McKendree College gave him the honorary title of D. D. At the General Conference of 1844 at New York City, he resisted to the utmost of his ability the division of the denomination (over the slavery issue) into the Methodist Church North and the Methodist Church south. He also struggled hard against those tendencies in the church, by which the merely itinerant character of its clergy was largely laid aside for the more stable and fixed salaries of local pastorates. Cartwright was known for many years as an inflexible opponent of slavery.

In 1846 he ran for Congress against Abraham Lincoln and this time he was defeated. He had charged Lincoln with infidelism. Lincoln once attended a Cartwright meeting and at the conclusion the preacher asked all who wanted to go to heaven to stand. Lincoln remained seated, whereupon Cartwright asked where he wanted to go. "To Congress," honest Abe quietly responded. In 1853 Cartwright requested his conference area be assigned to him for the first time, the Pleasant Plains District, home territory, which was granted him. Now at age 68 weariness was beginning to take its toll. Many times he had to defend his life against Indians and wolves, sleep on the ground and swim the swollen rivers to make appointments. Once he started a training school where the tuition was $5 per month, if paid in advance; and if the students did not have the money, they could trade in produce. He himself had empathy with the poor. He never would have succeeded in the fashionable eastern churches, but was God's man for the frontier. Once while visiting Boston and preaching at a "high-falutin'" church, he arose as the organ peeled forth and said, "Stop that squealin' you have up there in the gallery. I will line the hymn. . .We don't worship God in the West by proxy or substitution." He rolled up his sleeves, unbuttoned his collar and went to work on the crowd.

In his autobiography written in his 72nd year (1856) Cartwright mentions some totals covering his 53 years of preaching up to that time. He had nine children, seven daughters and two sons. Besides the death of one previously mentioned, another married daughter had also died. By the time of Cartwright's death, he had 50 grandchildren, 36 great grandchildren, and 7 great great grandchildren.

He traveled eleven circuits, and twelve districts; received into the Methodist Episcopal church on probation and by letter 10,000; "baptized" 12,000 (children 8,000 and adults 4,000), preached 500 funerals, and about 14,600 sermons. He closed his autobiography lamenting the fact that the old fashioned camp meeting was getting to be a thing of the past as the Methodist Church had become numerous and wealthy. The Methodists increased across America from 72,784 to 1,756,000 members during his 50 years of preaching.

He did a bit of arming when not actively preaching and lived out his days in good health until old age took its toll.

In May 1868 he attended his last General Conference and said (age 83) "Yet if after you have listened to my few remarks, any of you can beat them, come up and try. . .A lazy minister is a curse to the church of God. . .Ministers are raised in hot houses now."

The Life
And Ministry Of

Christmas Evans
1766- 1838

CHRISTMAS EVANS

BORN: December 25, 1766   **DIED:** July 18, 1838
Ysgarwen, Wales   **Swansea, Wales**
Life Span 71 years, 6 months, 23 days

He had but one eye which was a brilliant star over against the ghastly empty socket on the other side of his face. "But, my soul, he could preach!" exclaimed B. H. Carroll to the students of Southwestern Baptist Theological Seminary. "Gentlemen! Gentlemen! I would rather be able to preach to lost souls like Christmas Evans did than to be the author of every speculative vagary since Epicurus died. . ." And preach he could!

We do not analyze sermons in these sketches --you must do that for yourself, and you would behold the naked demoniacs bounding out of tombs, see Jesus in the quiet of His majesty cast out demons with a word. But even this does not tell the story, for we miss seeing the throngs which heard Evans, falling to the ground as if rocked by an earthquake. Twice Wales was smitten with Holy Ghost power, once with Evans in the early 1800's and 100 years later by another--Evan Roberts.

Evans was born on Christmas day to a poor shoemaker, Samuel and his wife Johanna Evans. He was the first born that came to the rubble cottage and they thought of naming the child Vasover; but because of the day, they decided Christmas would be fitting. He was reared in poverty as were many greatly used preachers. When Christmas was nine, his father died in his cobbler stall with awl in his hand. For a short time, Joanna desperately tried to keep her little brood together; even "went on the county," but to no avail, and the children began to scatter. Christmas was sent to live with a farmer uncle, James Lewis, at Bwlcheg. And Uncle Jim was as mean as they come. Christmas was fed and clothed in return for his labor on the farm.

For the next seven years, following his uncle's footsteps, he ran with a gang of young mountain hoodlums. The uncle was a drunkard and Christmas was without a friend or anything that resembled a home. At age seventeen he could not read a word. During these years he was the subject of a number of serious accidents, narrowly escaping with his life. Once he was stabbed in a quarrel, once he nearly drowned, recovering with great difficulty; once he fell from a high tree with an open knife in his hand, and once a horse ran away with him, passing at full speed through a low and narrow passage.

At 17 he left his uncle and continued his farming elsewhere at Glanclettwr, Penyralltfawr, Gwenawli and Castellhywel. About this time he attended a church at Llwynrhydowain which was an Arminian Presbyterian Church. A revival took place in the church under David Davies, and many young people united with the church. Christmas states that God's grace followed him from that time on. He was awakened spiritually and born into God's family. This conversion was undoubtedly in 1784. Soon he amazed others by saying, "God has called me to preach." Davies was a school-teacher as well as a preacher, so Evans and others bought Bibles and candles and met together in the evening in a barn at Penyralltfawr and within one month he was able to read his Bible. He borrowed books and began to learn Welsh and English. He went to the local pastor's school for six months and went through the Latin Grammar. Evans became a servant to this Presbyterian pastor.

Evans renounced the society of profane drunkards, and his penitent return to godliness stirred up the wrath of his former friends. Six young ruffians attacked him with clubs one night as he made his way home on the mountain road from a church service. He was beaten with sticks and one blow landed on his forehead and destroyed his right eye leaving it sightless the rest of his life. The night following this heavy disaster Evans dreamed, "I saw Jesus in the clouds, and all the world on fire. Jesus said, 'Thou thoughtest to be a preacher. . .it is too late,' for the Day of Judgment is come." Still confused with sin and ignorance, he determined to be a preacher as a result of these incidents, losing his sight and having a vision of the end time. There appears to have been a law in the local church which stated no member of the church should be permitted to preach until he had passed through a college course. So, cottage preaching was where he began. Congregations assembled in those cottages became his training ground. His first sermon and prayer were borrowed. He became dissatisfied with his church as he heard other celebrated preachers with more grand, scriptural and evangelical truth. He became convinced about the true meaning and importance of baptism. So Evans joined the Baptist Church at Aberduar. This was June 1787 when he was 20 years old. He was baptized in a river by Rev. Timothy Thomas in 1788. He preached as doors opened for him. In 1790 at age 23, Christmas was ordained a Baptist minister at Lleyn in Gaernarvenshire and became pastor of his first church at the same place.

Lleyn was not even a village; it was a little inland hamlet out of Caernarven Bay. It was shut in by the sea and the mountains, a most desolate place to begin a ministry. He was actually ordained as a missionary to work among the humble churches in that vicinity. Here a new life of faith began to grow in him. A wondrous power attended his preaching and numbers were gathered into the church. Frequently his congregations bathed in tears and weeping. A remarkable revival of religious feeling woke up everywhere he went--churches, coal mines and open fields.

Seventeen ninety was also the year that he married Catherine Jones, who became a wonderful help mate. Still in her teens, she was tremendously dedicated. She would rather be the wife of Evans on a salary that never exceeded $85 per year than to be the Princess of Wales. On five of his evangelistic missions she would be right behind him on the same horse, typical of her being behind him in everything he did until she died 33 years later.

After a while he accepted an invitation to visit the more remote parts of South Wales. He could not obtain a horse so he walked the whole way, preaching in every village or town through which he passed. Very frequently large numbers would follow after him the next day and attend the services many miles apart. So he went through the counties of Cardigan, Pembroke, Caernarven, Glamorgan, Monmouth and Brecknock, stopping and holding services at innumerable villages lying in the way. Soon his name was sufficient to attract thousands to a given place. Still living at Lleyn, he served as an itinerant missionary and soon acquired a greater popularity than any other preacher in Wales. It was not uncommon for him to preach five times on Sunday and walk 20 miles to do it.

His first major impact upon the entire countryside was at a meeting held at Velinveel. Many were gathered in the open air. The tall, bony, haggard young man, uncouth and ill-dressed, showed up to attend this Association meeting. Evans was known in the North but not too well in the South; but from that day on, he was the most sought after speaker for the annual Baptist Association meetings. He was asked to speak. People and preachers skeptical of the one-eyed monstrosity were moved and soon cries of "glory" and "blessed" filled the air. Drawn from all over Wales, people went home talking about Christmas Evans.

In 1792 he felt a call to go to the Island of Anglesea where he served over all the Baptist Churches of the island. He left on his 26th birthday for this new and enlarged world of work. It was a rough day of snow and frost and "we, like Abraham, knew not whither we went. But we did know Him who said, 'I am thy exceeding great reward.'" Anglesea is 189 square miles of island off the northwest coast of Wales. A twenty-minute ferry was utilized to reach it from the mainland. Traveling on horseback, he counted ten small Baptist Societies lukewarm and faint. He was the only minister within 150 miles and so he went to work. He called for a day of fasting and prayer and soon began to see revival. He chose Llangefni to be his home and Cildwrn Chapel would be his headquarters. His home was poor and scanty, furniture was the same, the door was rotted with a tin plate across the bottom, the roof was so low that one had to exercise care when roaming through the premises. There was no separate room for study. Here he taught himself Hebrew and Greek. It was during this earlier period of his ministry that the Sandemanian controversy, which shook the churches and especially the Baptist churches, took place. Evans himself for a time fell under the power of this new philosophy. It was the adopting of rigid ritualistic conservatism as the primitive form of apostolic times and separation from all other Christian groups.

Evans soon spent time using sermons against Sandemanianism (extreme Calvinism), but he dried up as he was engaged in this controversy. His health failed, his ministerial joy departed and he remembered the days of Lleyn. Evans testified later that he was weary of a cold heart towards Christ and of His sacrifice and the work of His Spirit --of a cold heart in the pulpit, in secret prayer, and in the study. Lacking a horse, he departed by foot for South Wales "seeking what he had lost." As he passed through the mountain villages, he preached, "Jesus only and my poor heart began to be warm again." One day as he trudged between Dongelly and Macyulleth, climbing up towards Dadair Idris, he had to pray. The struggle lasted for hours. Then he felt the fetters loosening and his hard heart softening. Tears began to flow and the joy of his salvation returned. In his preaching the next day the Holy Ghost began to work everywhere. Thus, he had a deeper experience and immediately wrote down a thirteen-item covenant with God, initialing every one of the items. Two of them were as follows: 4. Grant that I may not be left to any foolish act (such as anti-Sandemanianism) that may occasion my gifts to wither and be rendered useless before my life ends. 8. Grant that I may experience the power of Thy word before I deliver it as Moses felt the power of his own rod before he saw it on the land and waters of Egypt.

This covenant was signed April 10, (year not certain) but perhaps around 1802 after the back of Sandemanianism was broken due to the stand of one Thnomas Jones, a grand preacher of Glynceirieg. In the next two years Evans' ten preaching places increased to twenty and 600 converts were added to the Church where he headquartered. The desert was rejoicing and the roses were beginning to bloom in Anglesea. The six-foot gargantuan continued to preach. Evans was described as "the tallest, stoutest, greatest man one ever saw. He appears like one composed on the day after a great battle out of the scattered members of the slain. An anak whose head is covered with thick, coarse, black hair. His gait unwieldy, his limbs unequal and the one eye. . ." Evans would give out some verses of a well-known Welsh hymn; and while it was being sung, take out a small vial from his waistcoat-pocket wetting the tips of his fingers and drawing them over his blind eye. He was using laudanum to help deaden an excruciating pain which, upon some occasions, possessed him. So he continued on horseback or on foot, sometimes through the countryside frowning, sometimes laughing in hot summer and cold winter to fulfil his engagements.

His preaching was so eloquent that it was said that once when he was preaching on the subject of the Prodigal son, he pointed to a distant mountain as he described the father seeing him while yet a great way off, whereupon thousands in his congregation turned their heads in evident expectation of seeing the son actually coming down the hills. Evans' audiences alternately laughed and wept. Shouts of prayer and praise mingled together. One witness said the people seemed like the inhabitants of a city which had been shaken by an earthquake, that in their escape rushed into the streets, fell upon the earth screaming and calling upon God!

He had a famous sermon called the "Graveyard Sermon," in which he described the world as dead and buried in the graveyard of Law, with Justice guarding the gates but Mercy coming to unlock them. The preaching of it brought conviction of sin like a flood over the people. His appearance in a town would wake up a sleepy village, bid their inhabitants to pour along up by the hills and down by the valleys, the expectant crowds watching his appearance with shouts.

He was always able to think of ways to have a good collection. Once the money came in very slowly although the audiences were very large. At this time there was much sheep-stealing in the neighborhood. Evans told the people that undoubtedly some of the sheep-stealers must be present in the congregation, and he hoped that they would not throw any money into the collection. A big collection followed, with some people borrowing from their neighbors to contribute. Many of the chapels had pastors and all looked to Evans for guidance. He had a perpetual financial burden which he carried all during this time, for though the chapels multiplied and enlarged, Evans seemed to be the only person upon whom the burden of paying for them came. Often he would have to go forth into the south of Wales to beg from the righer churches for help. His sermons were often composed on the long, toilsome travels on his horse. In this way, he travelled from North to South Wales at least forty times; preaching always once every day in the week and twice on the Lord's Day. Some began to criticize and say he came too often. It was only the marvelous attractions of the messenger and message that saved him from some refusals.

He believed no missionary had to bear the burden he did with finances, for whereas London societies cared for their missionaries, Evans had to bear the burden of his own support and also that for all the chapel debts. Younger inexperienced ministers threw their responsibility upon him for after most efforts there remained large sums unpaid in connection with some of the chapels which had been built without his consent.

A big loss was the death of his wife in 1823. The couple never had had any children and her devotion to Christ is a story in itself. She constantly found food to give to poor children and needy people. She made clothes for the poor members and families of the church. She never had robust health but was always cheerful. She had a long illness and breathed her last saying, "Lord Jesus, have mercy upon me!" Evans' tears nearly destroyed his remaining eye and he wondered how he could escape sorrow unto death himself. But preaching renewed him and helped him forget his afflictions.

It appears that towards the close of the Anglesea period in 1826 he was thrown into a panic of fear by a threat of legal persecution on account of some chapel debts of which he was regarded as responsible. Now approaching his 60th year, the toil was beginning to take its toll. Only much prayer brought him through this problem. However, internal problems now became the next hurdle to face. The chapels which grew under his guidance began to refuse his advice in reference to ministers he suggested and invited others whose appointments he thought unwise. Now some of the people began to withhold their contributions to avenge themselves on their own father in the Gospel. Ingratitude after 34 years of service hardly seems possible; but thus it was and so, with sorrow in his heart, he moved on to Caerphilly. Jonathan Edwards had also suffered a similar fate--ingratitude and dismissal. In Evans' case he just left with a broken heart in 1826.

Summing up his ministry at Anglesea, he was a powerful preacher and a rigid disciplinarian. Many new chapels were erected and financed through annual drives he made each year all over Wales. Those were difficult journeys to say the least. His eye injury troubled him continually and at times threatened him with total blindness.

A Baptist church at Tenyvelin in Caerphilly then called him. It was a long, lonely journey of 200 miles to his new post. News spread throughout the area that Christmas Evans had come. He settled in the chapel-house. Soon Mary Evans, an old faithful servant of the Evanses in their earlier days, became his wife and serve him faithfully until he died. This second marriage was performed in the same church in which George Whitefield was married

(Eglwysilian in Glamorganshire). This was in 1826 or 1827. Every week many would come from all directions and the neighborhood re-echoed his sermons as they would be discussed in hundreds of homes. His body now was having infirmities, his one eye getting weaker. Again difficulties with the membership here caused him to transfer to Cardiff in 1828. On April 24, 1829, he made his second covenant with God by listing fifteen articles revised from his former ovenant. His temperament continued to dog him for this chapel's constitution was too democratic. He encourtered further opposition and made his final change to Caernarven in 1832. The church had only 30 members and was in disarray like the church at Lleyn when he began his ministry. But it was back in the northland where he felt a little more comfortable. After a seven year absence, he returned to Anglesea where he was received with much more appreciation and honor than at the moment of his departure.

The work at Caernarven was difficult. The people were poor and the congregation small. Drunkedness of some and pressure of debts were discouraging. So now, even though 71 years of age, Evans started on a tour throughout the south to attempt to raise money as he did so many times before. It was April of 1838. His wife and a young preacher, John Hughes, went with him. He had three months to live. He was received cordially and with great joy everywhere. His popularity was as great as ever. Crowds gathered at an early hour and often many could not get into the meeting places. He was laid up for a week at Monmeuthshire. He preached at various cities arriving at Swansea on July 14. On Sunday, the 15th, he preached twice at the Welsh Baptist Church, his sermons being on the Prodigal son and Romans 1:16. On Monday, July 16, he preached in Mount Pleasant Chapel, preaching in English which was always more difficult for him than his native tongue.

Evans had ridden his horse Jack through Wales for 27 years. In barren mountains alone with Jack he frequently talked to the horse. The animal became old in his master's service, knew at a distance his voice and lifted up his head when Christmas began to speak. And so he hitched Jack at the rail for his last service that Monday night and mounted the pulpit stairs. He preached on "Beginning at Jerusalem." After two hours he came down, desperately ill, and said, "This is my last sermon!" Illness came during the night that was to take him in a few days. He said to friends at his bedside, "Don't weep for me! I have laboured in the sanctuary fifty-three years and this is my comfort that I have never laboured without blood in the basin." "Preach Christ to the people, brethren. Look at me: in myself I am nothing but ruin, but in Christ I am heaven and salvation." He repeated a favorite verse of a Welsh hymn and then waved his hand and said, "Good-Bye! Drive on!" With his mind wandering back through the years, he gasped out, "Drive on, Jack, back! We have only to cross one low mountain, and then there will be oats, excellent water and a good stable. Drive on." The worthy shelter he desired for his horse was now his.

He left behind some sermons, tracts and hymns. He has been called the "Bunyan of Wales." He will not soon be forgotten. A large funeral in Swansea followed. He was buried in the ground attached to the Welsh Baptist Chapel there.

The Life
And Ministry Of

Charles Grandison Finney
1792 ~ 1875

CHARLES GRANDISON FINNEY

BORN: August 29, 1792
Warren, Connecticut

DIED: August 16, 1875
Oberlin, Ohio

LIFE SPAN: 82 years, 11 months, 17 days

Finney had as much power with God, power of God and power from God as any man that ever lived. When he got converted, he got whatever there is to get and got it 110%. During one revival (Utica, N.Y.) his very presence in town brought a conviction upon people who were not even at the meetings; and reports of people in lodging places calling upon God to save them defy any human explanation.

Born of parents Sylvester Finney and Rebecca (Rich), Finney spent his first two years in the wilds at Warren. The father had been a soldier in the Revolutionary War. In 1794, at age two, the family moved by ox train into the midst of the Oneida Indians at Hanover, New York. Here Charles received several years of frontier schooling, two of which were spent in the Indian Institute, known as the Hamilton Oneida Institute at Clinton. The ox train creaked again, and the family reached Henderson, 87 miles northwest in the wilderness near Lake Ontario in 1808. From 1808 to 1812 Finney trod the forests and taught in a district school before his family sent him back east to complete his education. Finney spent two years (1813-1815) in Warren, Connecticut, at an academy and was discouraged from entering into Yale, as a tutor told him he was bright enough to educate himself at less expense. He went to New Jersey, probably Hoboken, where he taught school from 1815 to 1817; and then he returned home to Henderson. In 1818 he entered the law office of Judge Benjamin Wright in Adams, New York. This town is 65 miles northwest of Utica and was ten miles from Henderson. As he read Blackstone's four commentaries on law, he noted many references to "the holy scriptures." Finney finally bought a Bible. After several weeks, he became convinced that the Bible was not to blame for the inconsistencies he saw among the religious people he knew. He was admitted to the bar in 1820.

At Adams, Pastor George Gale took it for granted that the hearers were theologians and left Finney perplexed as he attended the Presbyterian church. He soon joined and because of his musical background, was asked to be the choir director at the church. The pastor and lawyer became good friends, even though they did not understand each other. Gale was "hyper-Calvinist" and Finney found it hard to get his questions answered. He also saw an inconsistency between the prayers of Christians and the lack of answers. They prayed for a revival of religion and nothing happened.

However, a small band of the church young people prayed for him, led by 17 year old Lydia Andrews who had a burden for him for more than one reason.

On Sunday, October 7, 1821, he made up his mind that he would settle the question of his soul's salvation at once; and if it were possible, he would make his peace with God. That night before he went to bed, he cried out, "O God, I promise that I am going to give my heart to Thee." On Monday, October 8, he spent much of the day reading his Bible and engaging in prayer. On Tuesday, October 9, the conditions were the same, with much time to meditate because they were going to move their offices on Wednesday. By Tuesday night, sleep was denied him. Wednesday, October 10, came and his emotions were so aroused that he stopped dead still in the street as a Voice said, "Will you accept salvation now, today?" "Yes," he cried. "I will accept it today or die in the attempt." Instead of going to the office, he walked north of Adams on the country road to a favorite tract of timber. He penetrated into the woodland a quarter mile before he stopped. He knelt down to pray but couldn't. A gust of wind blew some leaves and he thought "someone is coming." He jumped up in panic. Now he was overwhelmed with a sense of his wickedness in being ashamed to have a human being see him on his knees before God. He broke down utterly and "began to cry at the top of his voice for mercy." He "became so full, he leaped to his feet, ran up the hill through the woods to the road and walked to the village."

Morning was gone and it was now noon. All sense of sin and guilt was gone. His afternoon was spent moving the office furniture to the new location. The Judge went home for the night, and Finney built a fire in the fireplace. His heart again seemed broken. Going into a back room, it seemed as if he met the Lord Jesus Christ face to face. Going back to the front office, he found the large oak logs he had put on the fire were burned out. Several hours had passed unknowingly. At that instant the Holy Spirit descended on him like a wave of electricity: "like waves of liquid love" he could feel the Spirit go through him, body and soul. At age 29, Finney had met the Master.

On Thursday, October 11, he woke late in the morning. He remembered what he had said the day before, "If ever I am saved, I will preach the Gospel." The question came to him, "Should I give up the legal profession?" Suddenly the answer came; he no longer had any desire to practice law. He went to his office and the senior partner, Judge Wright, arrived. Finney said a few words about his conversion. Wright looked with astonishment, made no reply, left the office. The remarks pierced him like a sword, and he did not recover until he was converted. A few minutes later a deacon came in. "Mr. Finney," he said, "my case is to be tried this morning. Are you ready?" Finney calmly replied, "I have a retainer from the Lord Jesus Christ to plead His cause and I cannot plead yours." He told the deacon how he was saved and about his decision to become a minister. The deacon dropped his head, went out and stood in the middle of the road for half an hour in deep meditation.

After Finney saw the old deacon rooted in the road, he closed the office door behind him and went up and down the village street like a salesman seeking customers conversing with any whom he might meet. His first stop was in the shop of a Christian shoemaker who was in conversation with a young man defending Universalism. His arguments were demolished and that evening the young man came back to town with a radiant testimony.

Without any invitation, the people of Adams that night made their way to

47

the Presbyterian Church. No one seemed ready to open the meeting, but the church was filled to capacity. Finney did not wait for anybody but simply rose and gave his testimony. A fellow lawyer left the service saying, "he is earnest but deranged." Pastor Gale arose and confessed he had not faith to believe that Finney would be converted.

Finney tirelessly began to testify everywhere. The impact spread out through the village and into the countryside. For a week he did not feel at all inclined to eat or sleep. Soon thereafter Finney went to Henderson and led his father and mother to the lord.

In order to learn enough theology to pass an examination before the local presbytery, he studied for two years with his pastor. While studying, he also preached in the vicinity and converted many of his friends and neighbors. This association with Gale as teacher-student that began in the spring of 1822 often ended up in controversy. He did not believe in writing his sermons. He disliked all illustrations that were not homespun. He made outlines after he preached, not before. His practice was to meditate for hours upon a text and the best way to apply it "until at last it went through him like a bolt of lightning." He received a license to preach from the St. Lawrence Presbytery on December 30, 1823, rather grudgingly. On March 17, 1824, in Utica he was appointed by the Female Missionary Society of the Western District of the State of New York "a missionary to labor in the Northern parts of the county of Jefferson and such other destitute places in the vicinity as his discretion shall dictate. . ." His salary was $600 per year. He worked as their missionary for two years.

He had heard of Evans Mills, 25 miles northwest of Adams. This frontier village was known for godlessness and opposition to religion. Bad men call it "Hell's Acres." By 1823 all religious meetings had been abandoned by the community. Finney, looking for a challenge, rode into town on March 22. On the last Sunday in March Finney preached there. On the first Sunday in April he was in Antwerp. Back and forth he went between the two towns, 16 miles apart; and by the first of May, a revival had broken out in both towns. He spent many hours each day calling on people under conviction, riding his horse Dash from one town to the other in ever widening circles through the forests to other communities. On July 11, the Presbytery grudgingly ordained him in the school house at Evans Mills. In one of these early revivals he preached in a village (near Evans Mills) whose nickname was Sodom where the only good man in town was named Lot. He invited Finney to hold the meetings. However, Finney was not aware of the nickname nor the name of his host friend. So on opening night he chose as his text "the destruction of Sodom and Gomorah." The local township was enraged but came back; and before the week was over, a great revival was held.

On October 9, 1824, he married Lydia Andrews in Whitestown. He had re-met her in March in Utica although she was originally from Adams. He went to Evans Mills for a second series of revival services with the thought that he would return home within a week in order to bring his bride to his new field of labor. The revival spread into various places so that Finney was prevailed upon to spend some time in small settlements such as Perch River, Brownville and Gouverneur, so that he had to write to Lydia of his delays. Finally on his way home for her in March of 1825, he was delayed by a revival at LeRayville, just a tiny place south of Evans Mills where he had stopped to have his horse sharp-shod. The power of God came upon the place so he continued his meetings day after day and finally sent somebody else to fetch her with his horse and buggy. A few days' absence after their marriage had turned into six months. The 20 year old bride and the 32 year old groom were seldom separated thereafter. Another association of Finney's was Father Nash, a backslidden Presbyterian preacher who traveled with Finney as his prayer partner from 1824 to 1927. He was revived in Evans Mills.

It was not until his revival in the town of Western in September 1825 that eastern newspapers began to carry reprints from the upstate New York papers about him. Finney rose from local to national fame in the years 1825 to 1827 as, following his Western crusade, he preached revivals in Rome, Utica, Auburn and Troy. In late 1825 in Rome he stated, "Convictions were so deep and universal that we would sometimes go into a house and find some in a kneeling posture and some prostrate on the floor. Some bathed the temples of their friends with camphor and rubbed them to keep them from fainting and, as they feared, from dying."

In the 1826 Utica crusade he visited a factory; and as the girls looked at him or he walked by them as they were busy with their work, their eyes began to fill with tears. Here and there sobs were heard and finally the owner closed the mill and a revival broke out in the factory with every worker being converted.

In Auburn, after hearing Finney, a young and prosperous distiller in Auburn went to his warehouse, broke open the casks and let the liquor flow into the streets.

In late 1826 the new measures and emotional excesses, which Finney was using to promote revivalism, were a direct challenge to those with old measures and little success. Opponents of Finney felt they needed the help from New England leaders of Congregationalism before this new approach would destroy the stability and good name of the churches. So Lyman Beecher and Asahel Nettleton were asked to help. In December of 1826 when Finney was at Utica, New York, Nettleton wrote many letters to pastors warning them of Finney's methods and disorders. On July 18 to July 27, 1827, Beecher and eight friends met Finney and eight of his friends at New Lebanon, New York, to debate issues but ended up bickering about "new measures." Neither side could claim a victory so both sides did. His ability to hold his own with Beecher made him more popular than ever and now the cities from the east were clamoring for him to see just what he was and did. In the fall of 1827 he decided to answer calls in the east and reach out from New York State. His last small town revival was in Stephantown. Wilmington, Delaware, was the first stop in November. He had to completely undo the pastor's views as he had done to his own Pastor Gale's.

Finney went on to Philadelphia, the center of Presbyterianism. He began his preaching on the outskirts of the city, but soon he was invited to speak in several of the leading pulpits downtown. He soon was preaching in the largest German Reformed Church in the city. Finney stayed in Philadelphia for a full year (early 1828-early 1829). It is said that some of the lumberjack converts of the Philadelphia meeting took the gospel upstream 80 miles to lumber camps in the backwoods areas many miles distant with 5,000 finding Christ as a result. He then went to Reading and Lancaster, Pennsylvania, and Columbia, New York. In the fall of 1829 Finney went to New York City and held a revival at the Vandevanter Street Church, preaching for three months. Then a former Universalist church on Prince Street was purchased and Finney continued to hold meetings there until midsummer of 1830. A sufficient number of converts were made to form a church devoted to Finney's principles. It was called the First Free Presbyterian Church. After a summer vacation in 1830, Finney intended to return to New York City to follow up his inroads when, at a sudden impulse, he decided to go to Rochester where he had been invited.

The Rochester revival was his most successful and widely publicized revival of all time. It might be the first such called "city-wide revival." The population was 10,000; and when it was all over, some 1,000 were converted and some 1,200 added to the city's three Presbyterian churches, including many lawyers, judges, physicians and other professional men. Forty lawyers went into the ministry. His methods and manner had matured during his recent years in the East. Now he was using logic, gravity and dignity but it was still revival preaching. This revival went from September 10, 1830, to March 6, 1831. Finney preached three times on Sunday and three evenings a week at the Third Presbyterian Church. The revival spread far beyond Rochester as revivalists and pastors who visited the city carried its enthusiasm and message back to the surrounding towns. A wave of revivals broke out from New England to Ohio. Five years later Finney claimed that 100,000 persons had been added to the churches as a result of the spark.

In July 1831 he went to Providence, Rhode Island, following Auburn and Buffalo, New York, crusades and preached for a short time. Then, after the most minute maneuvering, Beecher was forced to join with other ministers in inviting him to come to Boston. So from August 1831 to April 1832, Finney was in Boston preaching in many churches including Beecher's.

Finney decided to take a call to a pastorate in New York City, feeling he could have great influence there. The church was the Chatham Street Chapel or the Second Free Presbyterian Church. He began his New York work on April 29, 1832, meeting in a renovated theater seating 2,500 to 3,000 people. His salary was $1500 per year. The three galleries and orchestra of the theatre were thronged with worshippers. A group of men decided to build a tabernacle and invite Finney to be the pastor. But he did not want a fancy edifice. A simple tabernacle was built over the objections of the architect. The men also wanted the new church to be a Congregational Church. Finney concurred and changed his affiliation, not because of doctrine, but because he craved the independence of the Congregational democracy. He was installed as pastor of the The Chatham Street Chapel in New York City on October 5, 1833.

In January 1834 he was compelled for health reasons to take an ocean voyage. For six months he cruised about the Mediterranean, spending weeks at such places as Malta and Sicily. The Broadway Tabernacle would be erected for him upon his return. Sailing home on the mid-Atlantic in July, the Lord did a new work in his heart. It was fortunate that it so happened, for when he arrived home, he was greeted with the news that the Broadway Tabernacle had been gutted by fire just as it neared completion. He went to the cool uplands of Connecticut the rest of the summer and in the fall of 1834 came back to begin preaching in the stuffy Chatham Street Theatre for another year. The crowds also returned. He started on Friday nights to preach his "Revival Lectures." In 1835 Finney published his *Lectures on Revivals.*

On March 2, 1836, the switch was made to the new Broadway Tabernacle and Congregationalism. About this time Oberlin College (seating 2,500) in Oberlin, Ohio, came into focus. A small school was started there in 1834; but when Lane Seminary of Cincinnati split (trustees had asked students not to debate the slavery issue), the soon-to-be President of Oberlin, Asa Mahan, rushed to New York and buttonholed Finney with a proposition. Simply stated, many of the Lane students said that they would go to Oberlin if Finney would begin a department of Theology and teach. The school had 500 acres of land and 100 students already enrolled. The challenge was enticing, but he did not want to leave New York. Hence he spent his summers at Oberlin and his winters in New York for three years, 1835 to 1837, before relocating permanently in Oberlin in 1837. As the Lord worked it out, the pastor of the Congregational Church of Oberlin had resigned and Finney accepted on April 6, 1837, that pastorship which he was to hold the most of his remaining days.

He was also the head of the Department of Theology at Oberlin. He was also president of Oberlin from 1851 to 1866. Thousands flocked to "matriculate on the frontier," during his days there. His first year as president saw enrollment go from 571 to 1,070.

The church built a 1,000 seat auditorium and a great membership. The town had 4,000 population and the church was in continuous revival until Finney's resignation in 1872. By 1860 the membership was 1,545 and a second church was organized.

In the 1840's he held revivals in Providence, Boston, (2 times) Rochester, Cleveland, Cincinnati and Detroit during his winter vacations from Oberlin. In the 1850's he held meetings in New York, Brooklyn, Rochester, Hartford, Syracuse, Boston (3 times) and Charlestown. He also made two extended tours of various cities in the British Isles in 1849-50 and 1859-60 in connection with the prayer revivals. Some 500,000 were converted under his ministry. He edited a paper called the *Oberlin Evangelist* for many years. His sermons were printed therein 1839-1862.

In 1847 his wife Lydia and new-born baby Sara died. Four Finney children lived to maturity; Julia (born 1837) who married a James Monroe (teacher at Oberlin) and lived until 1930; Charles G., Jr. (attorney in California); Fred (railway work in Wisconsin) and Helen. A daughter Delia was born in 1844 and died at age 8. In 1848 he married Mrs. Elizabeth

Atkinson.

In 1863 death claimed his second wife Elizabeth; and in 1864, he married Mrs. Rebecca Helen Rayl, who died September 12, 1907, in Kentland, Indiana.

His closing days at Oberlin, 1872 to 1875, were filled with student contacts, anointed preaching and within 13 days of his 83rd birthday, he passed on one dawn following a night of suffering a heart attack.

His writings besides the *Revival Lectures (1851)*, which had a wide sale, were *Lectures on Systematic Theology (1876), Lectures to Professing Christians* and his *Autobiography (1846-47)* and *The Heart of Truth (1840)*.

The Life
And Ministry Of

Mordecai Fowler Ham
1877 ~ 1961

MORDECAI FOWLER HAM

BORN: April 2, 1877
Scottsville, Kentucky

DIED: November 1, 1961
Pewel Valley, Kentucky

LIFE SPAN: 84 years, 6 months, 29 days

Mordecai Ham's most famous convert was Billy Graham, one of 303,387 people brought to Jesus Christ through his crusades. Included were preachers such as John Wimbish and Grady Wilson, Judge Jenkins (Truett's father-in-law), plus scores of the hardened sinner type.

Ham's career in evangelism stretched from 1902 to 1927 and 1929 to 1961. It was in November 1934 that a sixteen year old boy went forward in the Charlotte, North Carolina, crusade. Little did Graham realize at that time that he would be preaching to multitudes one day.

Ham was the son of Tobias and Ollie (McElroy) and was born on a farm in Allen County near Scottsville. He came from eight generations of Baptist preachers. In 1886 his family moved to Bowling Green staying till 1888 when they returned to a second farm near Greenwood in Warren County. His conversion and spiritual inclinations were attributed to the devotional habits of his boyhood home. He cannot date his conversion. He stated, "From the time I was eight years old, I never thought of myself as anything but a Christian. At nine I had definite convictions that the Lord wanted me to preach. . ." At sixteen he was Sunday School Superintendent of the family church at Greenwood.

From country school, young Ham went to Ogen College (later Western Kentucky State Teacher's College) in Bowling Green, also studying law with a private tutor. Because he was too young for a Bar examination, he took a job as a traveling salesman for a grocery concern. From 1897 to 1900 he was crew manager for a picture-enlarging firm with headquarters in Chicago. His grandfather's death on February 28, 1899, was a renewed call of God to start serving the Lord. He married Bessie Simmons in July 1900, and in December he quit his business and answered the call to preach. He gave his partner his entire share in the business, borrowing money to get started in the Lord's work.

For the first eight months of 1901 he carefully studied and prayerfully read his Bible. His first sermon was on the absolute Lordship of Jesus Christ. In September 1901, he accompanied his father to a meeting of the District Association at Bethlehem, near Scottsville, where his grandfather had pastored for over forty years. There he was put on the spot and asked to preach. When he finished, the congregation was praising God and someone invited him to speak in the First Baptist Church of Scottsville that very night. He was then asked to preach in Kentucky at the Mt. Gilead Baptist Church.

At this, his first revival, he established a pattern that was to follow him the rest of his days. He went after the biggest sinners in town and often saw them saved. He believed enough personal evangelism would produce mass results.

A typical story is that of Ham seeking out the most notorious sinner in a Southern town. Ham was directed to a certain cornfield. The infidel saw the feared preacher approaching and went into hiding. The evangelist began to hunt his prey and hearing suspicious sounds under a cornshock, hauled him out.

"What are you going to do with me?" the atheist quavered. Ham retorted, "I'm going to ask God to kill you!". . ."You don't believe God exists. If there is no God, then my prayers can't hurt you. But if there is a God, you deserve to die because you are making atheists out of your children and grandchildren." As the infidel begged him not to pray that way, Ham said, "Very well then. I shall ask God to save you." He was saved; and before the meeting was over, all of that infidel's family was baptized--forty of them!

At Mount Gilead he encountered two incidents he could never forget.

First, a strange power came over him to prepare him for an experience on the next day. It was much like that which Finney and Moody described. . .an almost unbelievable power from the Holy Spirit. Ham always preached in that power from then on. The next day came the other incident. It was a visit to a dying girl named Lulu. As she closed her eyes in death, he called to her, "Lulu, how is it?" A voice came back, not the voice of one living, but that of one who is in another world. He was never able to forget it. . ."Lost. . .lost. . .Oh. . .so dark; so dark!" His sermon, "And Sudden Death" was heard by thousands in the days ahead. When he closed out this crusade, he had sixty-six baptized and received a love offering of $34.00. This was the beginning of his career in evangelism. He was ordained back home at the Drake's Greek Baptist Church in Bowling Green.

While Ham was holding a meeting at Mount Zion, Kentucky, he ran into the type of opposition that was to follow him most of his career. On the second night of the meeting the moonshine crowd surrounded the church and threw rocks at the preachers. The leader threatened Ham with a long knife. Ham said, "Put up that knife, you coward. . . Now I'm going to ask the Lord either to convert you and your crowd or kill you." The bully died the next morning before Ham could get to his bedside. On the same day a neighborhood sawmill blew up and killed three others of the crowd. That night he announced he wanted everything that was stolen to be returned before God killed the rest of the tormentors. Everything was returned. Eighty were saved in his revival.

His first year ended with 339 conversions. In 1902, his second year as an evangelist, he had 934 additions. In January 1903, he took his first meeting outside of Kentucky when he went to the First Baptist Church of New Orleans, Louisiana. Here one man threatened to kill him if his daughter joined the church. He later came back and was converted after Ham warned him that God was going to kill him. Other great 1903 revivals were in Garland, Texas, and Russellville, Kentucky. A large meeting was held in Paducah, Kentucky, in January of 1904. His first revival to produce large results was in Jackson, Tennessee, in April 1905, where he had 1,500 additions. The whole area was shaken as Ham's fame was rising.

On December 4, 1905, his wife died, stricken with cerebral meningitis. He was shaken to the depths, losing some fifty pounds and in January 1906, he sailed abroad to tour the Holy Land, greatly upset by the course of events.

The Houston campaign of November 12, 1906, to March 1, 1907, was outstanding. Starting as a Baptist meeting, it soon became a city wide endeavor with 4,000 attending in a downtown skating rink. Enthusiasm swept throughout the city. Five hundred were converted during the first five weeks. Then came two issues to hurt the crusade--an "Apostolic Faith" movement started to infiltrate the revival with their "tongue" participation. Then a controversy concerning the enforcement of Sunday laws (closing of theatres and saloons, which was not enforced) detracted from the meeting and divided some of the sponsoring pastors closing the meeting prematurely.

The 1907 Asheville, North Carolina, crusade saw some of the big saloon men converted. Then it was Louisville, Kentucky, and Wilmington, North Carolina, where the liquor crowd fought him hard. One night a drunken desperado rushed into the church and threatened everybody with a gun. Ham jumped off the platform singing, *"Tell Mother I'll Be There,"* and by the time he reached the fellow, the Lord had knocked him down, and he was on the floor begging for mercy. He was gloriously saved as he threw down a liquor bottle, a pair of dice and a gun.

In August of 1907 he held a meeting at Pleasureville, Kentucky. His fame reached to the communities all around, including Eminence, seven miles distance. From here, a Dr. and Mrs. W. S. Smith and their fourteen year old daughter, Annie Laurie, attended the meetings. Ham had just turned thirty. Visiting in the home, the little girl took the preacher for a ride in the buggy. Before the meeting closed, he mentioned to Mrs. Smith he wanted to take her daughter with him to Europe as his wife! On June 3, 1908, the thirty-one year old evangelist married a beautiful girl of fifteen. Three days later the happy couple sailed for Naples, Italy. She traveled with her husband for the most part during his meetings, playing the piano often in his campaigns. They had three daughters--Martha Elizabeth on September 16, 1912; Dorothy on December 16, 1915; and Annie Laurie, Jr., born December 11, 1924. The marriage was very successful and her warm and encouraging spirit enabled him to shoulder burdens that few have had. They made their home in Anchorage, Kentucky (1909-1927), then two years in the pastorate at Oklahoma City, and after 1929, in Louisville, Kentucky. The mother-in-law, Mrs. W. S. Smith, lived over forty years of her life in their home, enabling Mrs. Ham to travel frequently with her husband.

In March 1908, the Mardi Gras of New Orleans proved an exciting time. Ham started his city-wide crusade during the corruption of this celebration. Three thousand were added to the local participating churches before it was all over. It is said this was the first time that New Orleans became Protestant conscious.

The Ham revival was the only other important thing happening besides the election of a pope during the year as far as the local townspeople were concerned. Thousands of Gospels of John were distributed and the Roman Catholics instructed their people to burn them. As a result of that crusade, the state legislature passed two reform bills: one that separated saloons from grocery stores, and another that killed race-track gambling. A drunken ex-steamboat captain entered Ham's hotel room waving a gun in his face, threatening to kill him. Ham got him down on his knees and prayed (with his eyes open). The man was saved.

In 1908 he was also back in Asheville for another meeting. On to Salisbury, North Carolina, where in May the State Prohibition election was to be held. The night before the election, he had to be escorted to and from the tabernacle by armed guard; and after the service, the men paraded through the streets all night shouting, "Hang Ham! Hang Ham!" As he left by train, a U.S. Marshall had to stand outside on the station platform holding two pistols pointed toward the crowd. A railroad detective sat by his berth all the way to Asheville and got saved.

In July 1910, he began a meeting in Gonzales, Texas, where one of the great hymns of all time was written, *Saved, Saved*. As Ham preached on the "Cities of Refuge," a man was sitting in the audience who had killed four men and despaired of ever being saved. Midway through the sermon, he jumped up from his seat and shouted, "Saved! Saved! Saved!" Jack Scofield was directing the choir and was so inspired that the next afternoon he sat outside the hotel and composed both the words and music for the hymn entitled, *Saved, Saved*. That night the tabernacle audience heard the song for the first time.

In April 1911, Ham held his first meeting in Fort Worth, Texas, sponsored by J. Frank Norris and the First Baptist Church. During the first half of 1912 he held other meetings in Texas. It was at a Waco crusade that his song leader, W. J. Ramsay, of Chattanooga joined him. Texas and Oklahoma continued to dominate these days. In January of 1916 he began a meeting in Corpus Christi, Texas, and as usual, hit liquor hard. He was assaulted in the lobby of his hotel. Ham deflected the blow with his Bible and another man rushed up saying, "You are under arrest for fighting." Nothing came of this. However, Justice Miles subpoenaed him to appear in court and give the sources of his information concerning corruption and law violation in Corpus Christi. Word that the evangelist might be arrested, placed under bond, and tried for contempt of court fired up 3,500 followers of the meetings. As a result, it was thrown out of court. Then the grand jury took up the attack and ordered his appearances. Three thousand people gathered outside to take the court house apart, so the trumped up charges were dismissed. He received constant threats of the kidnapping of his little girl.

Back at Fort Worth, on September 11, 1916, Ham was assaulted as he was leaving the Westbrook Hotel on his way to the tabernacle to preach. He was struck from behind on the back of the head with gashes cut into the side of his face. Leading up to this, the "wet" opposition harassed and crippled the work of the campaign by outrageous nuisance tactics. At the tabernacle where some 12,000 people assembled, the meeting was broken up by a procession of automobiles laden with yelling men, following a squad of policemen who pushed back the ushers and others who attempted to bar their entrance. The meeting ended in a near riot with Ham's crowd declaring war on the city administration.

In San Benite, Texas, in January of 1918, some soldiers broke into the Woodman Hall and put on a dance. They were angered because Ham refused the use of his tabernacle for a Red Cross rally when he heard a dance was to be part of the rally. Crazed with liquor, they marched into his tabernacle, seized him and started up the railroad tracks with a rope, a bucket of tar, and a sack of feathers. A detachment of cavalry from the nearest army base came to his rescue as the mayor wired Washington of the predicament. They were three miles down the track before they were overtaken.

In 1920 and 1921 he was back in Kentucky and Tennessee, eight months of 1921 spent in Nashville, Tennessee. From 1922 to 1925 he was in the Carolinas, Florida and Georgia. The 1924 Raleigh, North Carolina, meeting had 5,000 decisions for Christ. It was his persecution at Elizabeth City, North Carolina, later that fall that started a new thorn in the flesh (up to this time it was Ragsdale). Now it was a W. O. Saunders who compiled a viciously slanderous book entitled *The Book of Ham* and circulated it in the cities where the evangelist undertook to hold meetings. In April of 1925, Ham ministered in Burlington, North Carolina, as well as Greenville, South Carolina, where he had 3,000 additions. In 1926 and 1927 he had two meetings in Danville, Virginia, resulting in 4,000 additions.

His total results since starting to preach up through 1927 included 33,650 souls in Texas, 8,737 in Oklahoma, 12,043 in Kentucky, 10,013 in Tennessee, 26,475 in North Carolina, 9,500 in South Carolina and 4,385 in Virginia. Ham's team members varied through the years, but his closest associate was W. J. Ramscy, who from May 1912 through 1945 was his right hand man. He was an excellent choir director and counter balanced Ham's sternness with his sense of humor. It was thought that much of the success of Prohibition was attributed to the preaching of Billy Sunday and Mordecai Ham.

Ham turned to pastoring in 1927. It all started with a crusade in 1926 that won 888. He then went to London in the fall of that year. In the spring, upon returning to his friends in Oklahoma City to give a report, he was met at the train by forty of the leading laymen of the First Baptist Church. Their pastor had resigned and they entreated Ham to accept the pastorate. Ham said a unanimous vote by the congregation would clinch it. He had always made enemies and never dreamed of total support anywhere so it was with shock he received the news of a unanimous ballot. He became their pastor on June 19, 1927. His big fight at the time was against the American Association for the Advancement of Atheism. On August 3, as he was crossing the street, he was struck down by an automobile and dragged for half a block. Whether it was an accident or a deliberate plot by the enemies of Christ remained an unanswered question. He was knocked out of commission for six weeks with a skull fracture. Fourteen doctors cared for him. Members of his Bible class guarded his hospital room to keep out curious visitors. Back in the harness against atheism and modernism, prayer meeting crowds rose to 2,200. He campaigned hard and fast for Herbert Hoover in the 1928 election, the first and only time he allied himself with politics. On June 16, 1929, he resigned from the pastorate as the fires of evangelism burned in his soul.

The Hams moved to Louisville, and joined the Walnut Street Baptist Church late in 1929. He began campaigning in Jackson, Tennessee; Lubbock, Texas; Danville, Kentucky, and then in November-December of 1929, in Okmulgee, Oklahoma. Here a miracle happened. Meeting in a tabernacle on an icy, snowy night, the timbers creaked from the weight of the snow on the roof. During the message someone suggested they go to the First Baptist Church to finish the meeting. When the last person had left the building, the center section caved in with a roar, cutting down seats like a great knife! A great tragedy was averted as God spared his people.

Six crusades were held in 1931, witnessing 11,400 decisions for Christ. In Johnson City, Tennessee, in 1931, he led 2,500 to the Lord in a six week meeting after the Pastors' Conference had voted not to ask him to come.

Three outstanding conversions took place in the next three years to further confirm Mordecai Ham's ministry.

The 1932 crusade in Chattanooga saw Wyatt Larimore converted. He was the "king" of the local underworld. He had been in court for almost everything from minor traffic violations to first degree murder. He had more than 300 men working under him.

In January of 1933 Ham opened a campaign in Little Rock, Arkansas, where a man named Otto Sutton was saved. He was a wild, worldly, wicked and reckless heavyweight fighter at the time. He later became the pastor of the Valence Street Baptist Church of New Orleans, Louisiana.

It was in the Fall crusade in Charlotte, North Carolina, whre he was having a trying time that Billy Graham was saved. The place was a temporary tabernacle on Pecan Avenue on the outskirts of town. A total of 6,400 were saved at this crusade. Young Graham was amazed as he saw more than 5,000 filling every seat. The next night with Grady Wilson, he sat in the choir hoping to escape the evangelist's wrath. The evangelist's first words were, "There's a great sinner in this place tonight." Billy thought, "Mother's been telling him about me." That night he turned to Grady and said, "Let's go!" Graham was saved and later became the most renown evangelist in history.

Ham went on to Spartenburg, South Carolina, where he saw 8,500 making decisions for Christ! This was the largest crusade of his life.

The Ham-Ramsey tent revival of 1937 was launched in Louisville, Kentucky, lasting four months. Some 4,000 decisions for Christ were made. In 1939 he led a campaign in Jacksonville, Florida, where 2,000 a night came. In 1940 it was Minneapolis and St. Paul, Minnesota. His last campaigns in 1941 were in Decatur, Alabama; Murfreesboro and Nashville, Tennessee; and Denver, Colorado.

In 1935 Ham was honored with a D.D. degree from Bob Jones University. In 1936 he was elected president of the International Association of Christian Evangelists. His rugged pace continued until his sixty-fifth year, 1941 beginning his last year in tent and tabernacle campaigns.

From 1929 to 1941 he had seen some 168,550 decisions (new converts, backslidden church members reclaimed), in sixty one crusades in fifteen states. Southern Baptist churches benefited the most.

The last twenty years of his life he continued a vigorous schedule highlighted by his radio preaching and appearance in over 600 cities, often preaching three and four times a day. He started a network ministry in 1940 on the Southern Mutual Broadcsting hookup of some fifty stations. In 1947 he started publication of a paper bearing the title, "The Old Kentucky Home Revivalist."

A close observer said it well, "He exalts Christ and fights with all his might. Under his preaching I have seen murderers saved, drunkards converted, homes reunited, and men and women dedicating their lives for special service." Over 7,000 workers were saved or called into Christian work during his meetings.

Ham authored the books, *The Second Coming of Christ* and *Revelation*. Booklets bearing his titles are *Believing A Lie, Light on the Dance, The Jews,* and *The Sabbath Question.*

The Life
And Ministry Of

Robert Reynolds Jones
1883 ~ 1968

ROBERT REYNOLDS JONES
(Bob Jones, Sr.)

BORN: October 30, 1883   DIED: January 16, 1968
Shipperville, Alabama   Greenville, South Carolina
LIFE SPAN: 84 years, 2 months, 18 days

Fundamentalism's greatest fortress of the faith for years has been Bob Jones University. "Preacher boys" trained here have fanned over the world with a zeal seldom matched anywhere. The fabulous growth has put it in the top spot as far as enrollment is concerned amongst Christian colleges. Some 5,000 take training there annually. What produces such a school? Many things, but the indefatigable work of the founder, Bob Jones, Sr., surely can be considered as the key ingredient. One of the great evangelists of all time, (preached in 30 countries) Dr. Bob's contribution to Bible Christianity has seldom been matched. At age 40, he preached 12,000 sermons to some 15 million people with 300,000 converts.

Jones was the son of William Alexander and Georgia (Cree) Jones. The parents were farmers of Calvinistic convictions. He was the eleventh of twelve children, having eight sisters and three brothers. The family moved to the Dothan, Alabama, area shortly after his birth. Christian convictions were instilled in him by his parents and hard work on the farm gave him a challenge early in life to work.

He was converted at age eleven in a country Methodist church outside Dothan. The preacher was 80 years of age and the young lad was the first to go forward. Since age six he had desired to get this matter settled.

From the time of his conversion he began preaching publicly and was known as "the boy preacher." He preached to anyone who would listen. He became a good debater. He developed strong convictions and undaunted courage. Like Billy Sunday, his preaching was to be received because it would be on the level of the people. He demonstrated unusual ability at memorizing Scripture and recitation. For months he had made speeches at the Sunday School, displaying great knowledge of the Bible. At age twelve he was appointed Sunday School superintendent at this Methodist Church at Brannon's Stand. Being something of a child prodigy, he would gather children of the neighborhood and preach to them. One day he caught some older folk hiding behind the trees, listening to what was going on. From this point on his father began to take a deep interest in his oratorical powers. Clipping significant pieces from newspapers and asking young Jones to commit them to memory. When he reached 13 years of age, he built a brush arbor (outside shelter of brush, lattice work, trees, etc.); and out of this meeting place, two miles from home, came a church of 54 members where he preached for about a year, (age 14). His mother died that year also. By age 15 he was licensed and ordained by the Alabama Conference. At 16 he headed a circuit of five churches, including the little church he had started. He would often walk miles just for the opportunity of having a chance to preach. He received $25 a month for this ministry. More than 400 came into the churches by profession of faith that first year. Bob was now preaching all over southeast Alabama. He finished his formal education, which was disjointed in his earlier years, at Kinsey (Alabama) high school, 13 miles away from home. He worked his way through school, living in the home of the principal, J. C. Hammett. Graduated in 1899, the year his father died, young Jones entered Southern University (later Birmingham Southern) at Greensboro, Alabama, in 1901 where he attended until 1904. He studied Latin, math and science, continued his preaching and was ordained by Methodists in 1903, from whom he withdrew in latter years because of their drift from the fundamentals of the faith.

While in college, he kept on preaching, first every weekend somewhere with good results, then campaigns, holding weekend revivals during school and full time meetings in the summer. For three summers he held meetings in the state of Louisiana. Fearing no man that they could control, the Methodists passed a rule that no Methodist layman or preacher could preach or hold a religious service within the boundary of a Methodist pastor's circuit without that pastor's permission.

This, of course, did not stop such as Bob Jones or his predecessor of those days, Sam Jones. Bob was stirring up the entire state of Alabama as a young man when he discovered his throat was bothering him more and more. It was diagnosed as "tuberculosis of the throat." He also had double pneumonia, was malaria-prone, and was told he could not live ten years.

He went west where he did recover, being healed by the Lord of this difficulty. This when he was 21. The following year on October 24, 1905, he married Bernice Sheffield, only to have her die ten months later in August 1906 of tuberculosis. About January 1907 in Uniontown, Alabama, he met Mary Gaston Stollenwerck, who was converted in his meeting. On June 17, 1908, they were married. Their only child, Bob Jones, Jr., was born October 19, 1911. This did not change his lifestyle as Mrs. Jones traveled with him, taking a maid along to care for the child until he was six years old when he entered school in Montgomery.

Following the death of Sam Jones and during the hey-day of the Billy Sunday meetings, Bob Jones was raising a storm throughout the country himself. In 1908 (now 25) he held a crusade in his home town of Dothan where some city officials, several of whom had been converted, called a meeting of the City Council and closed the dispensary, eliminating intoxicating liquor. It was also in 1908 that he witnessed two outstanding conversions. In Abbeville, Alabama, a Robert Reynolds was converted. This was his father's buddy in battle for whom Jones was named. Then in Ozark, Alabama, he led a Dr. Dick Reynolds to the Lord. This was the doctor that attended his birth. Several states were utilizing his services in the next couple of years--Texas, California, Missouri, New York, Georgia. Before age 30, he had preached in 25 states. In 1911 he was greatly used in Atlanta, Georgia, which had two notable services--a "Women Only" service at the Forsyth theater on June 2 and a large gathering of "Men Only" at the city auditorium on his last Sunday afternoon. People were long talking about his sermon, *"The Secret Sins of*

Men." In 1915 great crusades were held in two small Indiana towns. Crawfordsville had merchants closing their stores during the hours of the services. They later commented that it was easier to collect for bills and preachers found it easier to get people to come to church. Over 4,000 women gathered to hear his famous sermon for them, *"The Modern Woman."* One of the most amazing stories of revival in history took place in Hartford City, Indiana, a city of 7,000. Before the meeting, the church membership was 1,500; after the meetings the churches had almost 4,000 members. On the last Sunday of the meetings, 1,600 joined the churches. Some 100 per night accepted Christ. Sunday movies were closed and the city voted dry and put out of business 16 saloons within two months of his campaign there. Some 4,000 had attended his last service--in a town of 7,000 population.

In 1916 Jones had good meetings in Joplin, Missouri. Going east he was in a small New York town, Gloversville, beginning April 8. The headlines of the April 13 newspaper said, "Bob Jones launches savage attack against saloons and liquor traffic." Jones had simply talked on the topic, *Some Problems of Home* to some 3,500 who had gathered. The next night he preached to 4,500 on *The Sins of Gloversville.* The six-week crusade held at the Tabernacle on Temple Street was sponsored by 12 churches. The total attendance was 175,000 with 1,780 deciding for Christ.

He closed the year out with a large tent crusade in New York City. He was front page copy of the *New York Herald* for more than a week. The tent, located on West 12th Street, was the scene of many victories. Another outstanding revival that had been conducted that year was at the City Auditorium in Lynchburg, Virginia. Nineteen seventeen found him in Quincy, Illinois, then in a good Zanesville, Ohio, crusade from February 18 to April 1. Seventeen churches participated. Total attendance was 266,000 with 3,284 signed convert cards. His closing day attendance was 18,000. A large tabernacle had been erected which seated 5,000. Bob pounded the altar so hard while preaching that he broke it. Noon shop meetings. meetings with students and women's meetings were all a part of this crusade. One of his greatest crusades was the one that followed in Grand Rapids, Michigan. Some 1,000 met him at the train and some 10,000 gathered in parade route while the procession went to the tabernacle where such as Mayor Tilma officially welcomed him. Fifteen thousand attended the opening service. In response to the first invitation given the next day, 568 walked the "sawdust trail." Schools closed early so that children might attend special sessions for them at 3 p.m. A Sunday School parade had 2,500 participants. Over 5,000 converts were made during his ministry there.

In July of 1919 a good crusade was held in Columbus, Ohio. Meetings were held under the Big Tent. In 1920 he was in Anniston, Alabama, at the Lyric Theater. On Sunday, August 29, 1920, Jones and William Jennings Bryan were featured in a great rally at Winona Lake (Indiana) Bible Conference. In 1921 Jones crusaded at Steubenville, Ohio. Seventeen preachers who sponsored the meeting early in the year attested to the good results at the large tabernacle erected near the business center of the city. The newspapers gave great coverage. More than 4,000 marched in the Sunday School parade.

His greatest crusade in his own opinion was that of the Montgomery, Alabama, meeting in 1921. Beginning on May 22, the headlines the next day tell the story: 'More than Five Thousand Held Spellbound by Eloquence of Splendid Evangelist: Hundreds Turned Away at Each Sunday Service: Sermons Not Sensational." His *"Sins of Men"* address to 5,000 men was perhaps his greatest meeting ever held, by his own admission. At the close of the service over 2,000 men started a great rush to the front to shake hands with him so that he was forced to rush back to the platform and appeal to the men not to create a panic, but to respond to the proposition to live right by holding up their hands. Meetings were held at a large wooden tabernacle erected near the business center which seated over 5,000. The building was crowded to capacity every night and many times there were hundreds standing around the outside of the tabernacle. It is estimated some 12,000 heard him the closing Sunday night in June. Average crowds were 10,000 nightly (total population 40,000).

He received an honorary D.D. degree by Muskingum College during this year. In the late fall of 1921 he held a large campaign in St. Petersburg, Florida. The tabernacle seated 5,000 and sometimes it was necessary to have two services in order to accommodate the crowds.

In 1927 (year the Bob Jones College was founded) Jones held two large crusades. One was in McKeesport, Pennsylvania, and the other in Andalusia, Alabama. Jones' meetings continued with great success into the 1930's and 1940's. In 1947 he held good crusades in Spartanburg, South Carolina, and Asheville, North Carolina. As many as 100 per night were saved in the former, with scores coming forward each night at the latter as well. In 1949 at Presque Isle, Maine, a town of 10,000, between 50 and 200 were saved each night. In June of that year he returned to Ottawa, Ontario, Canada, for a 15 day crusade. The chairman of the sponsoring committee was his convert from a Pittsburg revival 25 years previous. His friendship with John R. Rice was a mutual help to both men with Bob Jones often appearing at the Sword of the Lord Conferences and then making the *Sword of the Lord* required reading amongst the preacher boys at the college. Concerning evangelism, Jones once said:

> I never had a goal as most men set up goals. My only goal was to do the job at hand, and then to begin another. I never started out to be a big evangelist, a little evangelist, or any other kind of evangelist. I just started out to do the job the Lord had for me at the time.

Some 30 nations of the world were to hear him preach as well.

In 1952 and 1959 Bob Jones made round-the-world missionary tours. Then again in 1964 in connection with his 80th birthday, the Jones' were sent on a goodwill tour around the world, visiting 14 countries. By this time 850 missionaries in 90 countries had received their education at the school he started.

Perhaps he has been an evangelist longer than anyone in the history of the

Christian church. He was preaching at age 13 and continued into his 80's which would give him over 65 years in this chosen field. He averaged some 40,000 miles travel a year. His decisions for Christ run into the hundreds of thousands, with one report stating his greatest single service response being 6,000 decisions.

As years went by, Jones was beginning to get another burden --that of starting a Christian college for the common people with whom he worked every day. Many were the sad stories of sending children off to college and seeing them return with agnostic views. Sitting in a drug store in Kissimmee, Florida, in 1927, the idea hit him hard. "I'm going to start a school," he told his wife. A site was picked seven miles out of Panama City on St. Andrews Bay. The name of the campus site would be College Point, Florida.

On December 1, 1926, ground was broken. The name of the school was described:

> I was averse to calling our school the Bob Jones College. My friends overcame my aversion with the argument that the school would be called by that name because of my connection with it and to attempt to give it any other name would confuse the people.

Jones from the beginning, like other noble evangelists, poured his large income from evangelism back into the work and for years the operating expenses of the school were always current because of this generosity. Whitefield and his orphanage, Moody and his schools, are notable examples of this kind of dedication.

On September 12-14, 1947, the school opened with 88 students. The financial crash of 1929 hit Florida especially hard, and assets of one-half million were wiped out. Enrollment was limited to 300 at the Florida campus. A site in Cleveland, Tennessee, appealed because of a better geographic position. Old Centenary College (Methodist Girls' School) had been closed for seven years and the move was made to Cleveland, Tennessee, on June 1, 1933. Formal opening was September 1, and a new school year was to begin. In 1934 Jones took a prolonged absence to preach in such places as Ireland, Poland and several engagements in Michigan. During this time Bob Jones, Jr. got some good experience in running the school. A great benefactor in those early days was John Sephus Mack (died September 27, 1940) who contributed much financial assistance in the development of the college. He was the head of the Murphy stores and first met Jones at a revival in his home town, McKeesport, Pennsylvania. Coming late to the meeting, he was seated on the platform. Here he witnessed Jones' lips moving, "Help me get ahold of this crowd." Being a conservative Presbyterian, this kind of praying seemed a bit informal; but since then, Mack also talked to Jesus in this fashion. He also told the evangelist if he ever made any money, he would give it to Jones if he needed it. One hundred fifty thousand dollars for the building program subsequently followed. By 1946 they had expanded as much as they could in Cleveland. Additional property needed to expand was next to impossible to obtain.

The Church of God was greatly interested in the property and so it was sold to them for one and a half million dollars. Much business needed to be done and Jones was constantly traveling, tying up loose ends and preaching. He missed the Winecoff Hotel fire in Atlanta in 1946 by one night, having checked out of the ill-fated hotel one day earlier than anticipated (120 died in that inferno). It was finally agreed to move the plant to Greenville, South Carolina, where it was dedicated on Thanksgiving Day, November 27, 1947. At this stage the school changed its name to Bob Jones University; and Bob Jones, Jr. assumed the presidency of the same, with Jones Sr. becoming Chairman of the Board. Some 2,900 students were now attending. Through the years the school continued to grow with Bob Jones, Sr. playing an active role until his resignation as the Chairman of the Board of Trustees in April 1964. Currently the school handles 4,000 to 5,000 students annually--one third of this number being ministerial students. Over 30 countries are represented in the student body. The school has excelled in film teaching and production, Shakespearean drama productions has amassed one of the finest collections of religious paintings in North America. The $40 to $50 million assets with 180 some acres made the modern facilities and beautiful campus a legend amongst Christian schools.

Refusing to compromise in any way, shape or form the Bible principles established in the very beginning, the school has been coerced and criticized. The discipline and dramatics program have been misunderstood and derided. Because of its refusal to become a part of the Southern Association of Colleges and Secondary Schools, some have felt it to be unscholarly. Because of the monitoring of dates and the "six-inch rule" between opposite sexes, some have felt the school antiquated. Because of the school's refusal to back the Billy Graham New York Crusade in 1957, an attempt to discredit the school's leadership was made. The conclusion of all this is that Bob Jones the man and Bob Jones the school were just not going to change their stand. In the early days of Youth for Christ and the National Association of Evangelicals, Jones was a prime supporter. Once at an alumni meeting of his school, he asked all present to sign a pledge that they would use their influence to have the school closed if it ever developed modernistic leanings. Both the man and the school he started continued to prosper and history will show that a greater combination evangelist-educator never lived. When he was on campus, one of his main jobs was his "chapel talks" where students received character training and purpose. He left the Methodist Church in 1939.

Jones will be remembered as the man who was one of the first to take the unpopular stand in those days of opposing the policies of Billy Graham. So much has been blown out of proportion, but the simple facts are these. When Graham began to insist upon the total support of a city as he did in the famous 1957 New York crusade, Jones would not put aside convictions of a life time and ignore something he felt was harmful. Hence, he, John R. Rice and others decided the truths of II John 9-11 should be adhered to. It was not a personality clash as some would like to think. It was not a matter of jealousy for Jones promoted and supported Billy Graham until the fraternization with liberals started. The ecumenicity of Graham's new sponsorship resulting in the practice of returning converts to unscriptural churches and false teachers as well as sound churches and good teachers clashed with Dr. Bob's philosophy, "It is not right to do wrong to get a chance to do right." So the polarization of New Evangelicals and Fundamentalists did start for the most part in 1957 as this policy developed. Of course, the right kind of fundamentalist will rejoice in souls won by Graham or anyone else, as the issue is not a man--but a Biblical principle. Bob Jones and John R. Rice sponsored an historic meeting in Chicago on December 26, 1958, where some 150 prominent evangelists gathered to form resolutions backing historic Christian premises in the field of evangelism.

Muskingum College gave him a D.D. degree in 1921 and John Brown University granted Jones a LL.D. degree in 1941. A plaque in his honor was unveiled in Dothan, Alabama, on October 18, 1962, marking his birthplace. The Christian Hall of Fame in Canton, Ohio, honored him in 1966 as the only living entree in their portrait gallery of greats. The last two years of his life he was in the school hospital. His last words were, "Mary Gaston, get my shoes; I must go to preach." He was buried on campus in a beautiful little island in a fountain of cascading pools just across the street from the Rodeheaver Auditorium. An excellent biography of his life is the book *Builder of Bridges* by his friend of many years, R. K. Johnson.

The Life
And Ministry Of

Dwight Lyman Moody
1837 ~ 1899

DWIGHT LYMAN MOODY

BORN: February 5, 1837   **DIED:** December 22, 1899
Northfield Massachusetts   Northfield, Massachusetts
LIFE SPAN: 62 years, 10 months, 17 days

Dwight Lyman Moody was the first evangelist since Whitefield to shake two continents for God.

It was on his mother's birthday that Moody was born on a small New England farm. He was only four when his father, Edwin, a bricklayer and an alcoholic, died suddenly at 41. His mother, Betsy (Holton) was now a widow at 36 with seven children. . .the oldest being thirteen, and D. L. being the youngest. Twins were born one month after the death of the father bringing the total to nine. Their uncle and the local Unitarian pastor came to their aid at this time. The pastor also baptized Moody (age five) in 1842. This was undoubtedly sprinkling and his only "baptism" experience.

Six year old Moody never forgot seeing his brother Isaiah leave home. The reconciliation, years later, became an illustration in a sermon depicting God welcoming the wanderer home with outstretched arms. Moody's education totaled seven grades in a one-room school house; and during his teenage years, he worked on neighboring farms.

On his seventeenth birthday (1854), Dwight Moody went to Boston to seek employment. He became a clerk in Holton's Shoe Store, his uncle's enterprise. One of the work requirements was attendance at the Mount Vernon Congregational Church, pastored by Edward Kirk. Church seemed boring, but a faithful Sunday School teacher encouraged him along. One Saturday, April 21, 1855, the teacher Edward Kimball walked into the store and found Moody wrapping shoes. He said, "I want to tell you how much Christ loves you." Moody knelt down and was converted. Later he told how he felt, "I was in a new world. The birds sang sweeter, the sun shone brighter. I'd never known such peace." Not sure of his spiritual perception, it was a year before the church admitted him for membership!

On September 18, 1856, he arrived in Chicago where another uncle, Calvin, helped him obtain a position in a shoe store operated by the Wiswall brothers. His interest in church work continued as he joined the Plymouth Congregational Church. He rented four pews there to provide lonely boys like himself a place of worship. Then he joined the mission band of the First Methodist Church, visiting and distributing tracts at hotels an boarding houses. Here he met wealthy dry goods merchant John V. Farwell, who later would be a great help. He also worked out of the First Baptist Church where he was later married. The prayer revival that was sweeping the nation in 1857-59 also contributed to his enthusiasm for the things of God. Discovering a little afternoon Sunday School on the corner of Chicago and Wells, he offered his help. He was told there was already nearly as many teachers a students so he began recruiting. The first week he brought in eighteen students doubling the Sunday School! Soon his recruiting overflowed the place.

He withdrew to the shores of Lake Michigan in the summer of 1858 and taught children, using pieces of driftwood as chairs. He was dubbed "Crazy Moody" about this time, but respect came through the years as the title slowly changed to "Brother Moody," "Mr. Moody," and finally "D. L. Moody."

In the fall of 1858, he started his own Sunday School in an abandoned freight car then moved to an old vacant saloon on Michigan Street. A visiting preacher reported his favorable impressions. . .seeing Moody trying to light the building with a half dozen candles and then with a candle in one hand, a Bible in the other and a child on his knee teaching him about Jesus.

The school became so large that the former Mayor of Chicago gave him the hall over the city's North Market for his meetings rent free. Farwell visited the Sunday School and became the superintendent upon Moody's insistence. The use of prizes, free pony rides and picnics along with genuine love for children soon produced the largest Sunday School in Chicago, reaching some 1,500 weekly. Moody supervised, recruited and did the janitor work early Sunday morning, cleaning out the debris from a Saturday night dance to get ready for the afternoon Sunday School.

It was in June 1860 that Moody decided to abandon secular employment and go into the Lord's work full time. He was now 23 and in only five years had built his income up to $5,000 annually and had saved $7,000. Friends believed he could have become a millionaire had he concentrated his efforts in business. Income for the first year in his Christian ventures totaled no more than $300.

This decision was prompted by the following incident. A dying Sunday School teacher had to return east because of his health and was greatly concerned about the salvation of the girls in his class. Moody rented a carriage for him and the teacher and went to each girl's home winning them all to Christ. The next night the girls gathered together for a farewell prayer meeting to pray for the their sick teacher. This so moved Moody that soulwinning seemed to be the only important thing to do from then on. He made a vow to tell some person about the Savior each day, even though it eventually meant getting up out of bed at times.

On November 25, 1860, President-elect Abraham Lincoln visited Moody's Sunday School and gave a few remarks.

In 1861 he became a city missionary for the YMCA.

He married Emma Charlotte Revell on August 28, 1862, when he was 25 and she nineteen. The three Moody children were Emma (October 24, 1864), William Revell (March 25, 1869) and Paul Dwight (April 11, 1879).

With the advent of the Civil War, Moody found himself doing personal work among the soldiers. He was on battlefields on nine occasions serving with the U.S. Christian Commission. At the Battle of Murfreesboro in January 1863, under fire, he went among the wounded and dying asking, "Are you a Christian?"

During the Civil War, he was also back at his Sunday School from time to time where popular demand forced him to start a church. A vacant saloon was cleaned, rented and fixed up for Sunday evening services with the Sunday

School continuing at North Market Hall until it burned in 1862. Then Kinzie Hall was used for a year. In 1863, when only 26, he raised $20,000 to erect the Illinois Street Church with a seating capacity of 1,500. It began February 28, 1864, with twelve members. This was the official beginning of what is now known as Moody Church. He preached Sunday evenings until a pastor, J. H. Harwood, was called in 1866 and served until 1869, during which time Moody served as a deacon.

The Chicago Y.M.C.A. was moving ahead also as Moody rose to its presidency from 1866 to 1869. He had a part in erecting the first Y.M.C.A. building in America when he supervised the erection of Farwell Hall in 1867 seating 3,000. That year he also held his first revival campaign in Philadelphia.

In 1867, primarily due to his wife's asthma, the couple went to England. He also wanted to meet Spurgeon and Mueller. On this trip, while they sat in a public park in Dublin, Evangelist Henry Varley remarked, "The world has yet to see what God will do with and for and through and in and by the man who is fully consecrated to Him." John Knox allegedly originated this saying that was now to burn in Moody's soul (some historians put this Varley conversation in an 1872 trip). Moody met Henry Moorhouse also in Dublin and was promised a visit to Chicago.

Three incidents prepared Moody for his world famous evangelistic crusades. First, in February 1868, Moorhouse came as promised to Moody's pulpit in Chicago. For seven nights he preached from the text John 3:16, counseling Moody privately, "Teach what the Bible says, not your own words and show people how much God loves them." Moody's preaching was much more effective after that.

A second incident was the meeting of Ira A. Sankey while attending a Y.M.C.A. convention in Indianapolis in July of 1870. Moody was to speak at a 7 a.m. prayer meeting on a Sunday morning. Sankey was there. When Moody asked for a volunteer song, Sankey began to sing *There is a Fountain Filled With Blood*. Moody's direct approach was, "You will have to come to Chicago and help me. I've been looking for you for eight years!" Sankey left his post office job in Pennsylvania and joined Moody in Chicago in early 1871.

A third incident was the Chicago fire and the ensuing filling of the Holy Spirit. On Sunday night, October 8, 1871, while preaching at Farwell Hall, which was now being used because of the increased crowds, Moody asked his congregation to evaluate their relationships to Christ and return next week to make their decisions for Him. That crowd never regathered. While Sankey was singing a closing song, the din of fire trucks and church bells scattered them forever for Chicago was on fire. The Y.M.C.A. building, church and parsonage were all to be lost in the next 24 hours. The church was reopened on December 24, 1871, and it was now called the North Side Tabernacle, located on Ontario and Wells Street close to the former building. There was no regular pastor at this church in its brief history 1871-1876.

While out east raising funds for the rebuilding of this church, he describes a life-changing experience he had upon locking himself in a room of a friend's house. . ."one day in the city of New York, Oh what a day! I cannot describe it. I seldom refer to it, it's almost too sacred an experience to name. Paul had an experience of which he never spoke for fourteen years. I can only say that God was revealed to me and I had such an experience of His love that I had to ask Him to stay His hand. . ."

In 1872 he returned briefly to England where he accepted an invitation to the Arundel Square Congregational Church in London. The evening service ended with nearly the entire congregation in the inquiry room. He continued on for ten days with some 400 people saved. It was learned that an invalid had been praying for two years for him to come to the church!

Three English men invited him back the following year. With their families, Moody and Sankey left June 7, 1873. Little did they know that they were going to shake England as Whitefield and Wesley had 125 years previously. Two of the sponsors had died by the time they arrived and they were fortunate to get an invitation to conduct some meetings at the York Y.M.C.A. Five weeks of meetings saw 250 won to Christ. F. B. Meyer was the principal supporter. Then they traveled on to Sunderland for five weeks with Arthur A. Rees, the host. Next came Newcastle where the meetings were gigantic with special trains bringing people in from surrounding areas. Here a novel all-day meeting was held and their first hymn book was introduced to the public.

Now being invited to Scotland, the evangelists began in Edinburgh on November 23. For hundreds of years, only Psalms had been sung here with no musical instruments. Now Sankey began "singing the Gospel" and crowds packed out the 2,000 seat auditorium. By the time the last service was over on January 20, Moody was receiving requests from all over the British Isles. They spent two weeks in Dundee and then began the Glasgow, Scotland, crusade on February 8, 1874. These meetings soon moved into the 4,000 seat Crystal Palace and after three months, climaxed with a service at the famed Botanic Gardens Palace. Moody was unable to even enter the building surrounded by 15,000 to 30,000 people, so he spoke to them from a carriage and the choir sang from the roof of a nearby shed! Later the team returned to Edinburg for a May 24 meeting held on the slopes of "Arthur's Seat" with a crowd of 20,000. An estimated 3,500 converts were won in each of these two places.

Now Ireland was calling, so they began at Belfast on September 6, 1874. People flocked to hear them and the largest buildings of each city were used. A great climactic service was held in the Botanic Gardens on October 8 in the open air with thousands attending. One final service was held October 15 with admission by ticket only. Tickets were given only to those who wanted to be saved. Twenty-four hundred came. Next it was Dublin (October 26-November 29), where even the Irish Catholics were glad at the awakening amongst their Protestant neighbors. The Exhibition Hall seating 10,000 was filled night after night with an estimated 3,000 won to Christ.

Back in England on November 29, the Manchester crusade was held at the Free Trade Hall. No hall was large enough! As many as 15,000 were trying to gain admission for a single service. Next came Sheffield for two weeks beginning on December 31, then Birmingham with untold blessing. The January 17-29, 1875, crusade noon-day prayer meetings drew 3,000. Bingley Hall seated only 11,000 but crowds of 15,000 came nightly. Liverpool was next where the 8,000 seat Victoria Hall was used from February 7 to March 7.

Finally, it was the London Crusade climaxing the tour. It was a four-month encounter from March 9 to July 11. Five weeks of preaching began in the Agricultural Hall in the northern part of the city. Then he moved to the east side in the 9,000 seat Bow Road Hall for four weeks. Next came the west side in The Royal Haymarket Opera House. Often during this time, Moody would hold a 7:30 meeting with the poor on the east side and then shuttle over for a 9 p.m. service with the fashionable. Then on the south side of London he spoke for several weeks in the Victoria Theatre until a special tabernacle seating 8,000 was constructed on Camberwell Green where he finished this crusade. A total of two and one half million people attended! The awakening became world news and it was estimated that 5,000 came to Christ. A final preaching service was held in Liverpool on August 3 before sailing for America. He arrived home August 14 and hurried to Northfield to conduct a revival. His mother, many friends and relatives were saved there. Invitations for city-wide crusades were coming from many places in America now.

His first city-wide crusade in America was in Brooklyn beginning October 31, 1875, at the Clermont Avenue Rink, seating 7,000. Only non-church members could get admission tickets as 12,000 to 20,000 crowds were turned away. Over 2,000 converts resulted.

Next came Philadelphia starting on November 21 with nightly crowds of 12,000. The Philadelphia crusade was held at the unused Pennsylvania freight depot which John Wanamaker had purchased. It was located at Tenth and Market. His ushers were very well trained, capable of seating 1,000 people per minute and vacating the premises of some 13,000 in 4 minutes if needed. The doors were opened 1 1/2 hours early and in 10 minutes the 12,000 seats would be taken. On January 19, 1876, President Grant and some of his cabinet attended. Total attendance was 1,050,000 with 4,000 decisions for Christ.

Next it was the New York crusade running from February 7 to April 19, 1876. The meetings were held in the Great Roman Hippodrome on Madison Avenue, where the Madison Square Gardens now stands. Two large halls gave a combined seating attendance of 15,000. Moody had just turned 39 for this crusade. Some 6,000 decisions came as a result of his ten-week crusade. Three to five services a day were held with crowds up to 60,000 daily.

Back in Chicago, his beloved church was expanding. Property had been purchased on Chicago Avenue and LaSalle. Thousands of children contributed five cents each for a brick in the new building. The basement, roofed over, served as a meeting place for two years, then in 1876 the building was completed and open on June 1, 1876, and formally dedicated on July 16 with Moody preaching. It was now called the Chicago Avenue Church and W. J. Erdman was called as pastor.

The Chicago crusade started October 1, 1876, in a 10,000 seat tabernacle, closing out on January 16, 1877. The sixteen week crusade was held with estimates being from 2,500 to 10,000 converts. Moody never kept records of numbers of decisions, hence reports vary. The meetings were held in a temporary tabernacle erected on Farwell's companies property, located at Monroe and Franklin, which was converted to a wholesale store after the crusade.

The Boston crusade was held January 28 to May 1, 1877, in a tabernacle seating 6,000. The years 1877-78 saw many smaller towns in the New England states being reached. The years 1878-1879 saw Baltimore reached in 270 preaching engagements covering seven months. In 1879-80, it was six months in St. Louis where a notorious prisoner, Valentine Burke, was saved among others. In 1880-81 it was the Pacific coast, primarily San Francisco.

Moody went back to England in September 1881, returning home for the summer of 1881. He returned for an important student crusade at Cambridge University in the fall of 1882, then back to America, and returned the following fall for a crusade in London from November 4, 1882, to January 19, 1884, where some two million heard him in various auditoriums. Wilfred Grenfell was among those saved and young C. T. Studd was also won indirectly.

From 1884 on his crusades were smaller and limited to October to April. He spent his summer months in Northfield, Massachusetts, for study, rest, family and development of his schools.

From 1884-1886 he was in many of the smaller cities of the nation, remaining about three days in each place. In 1888-1889 he was on the Pacific coast from Vancouver to San Diego. In 1890 he held his second crusade in New York, in November and December.

A last trip was taken in 1891-92 to England, Scotland (99 towns), France, Rome and Palestine, where he preached on the Mount of Olives on Easter Sunday morning. On his trip home to America, he endured a shipwreck, a dark hour of his life, but God spared him.

Peter Bilhorn, who substituted for Sankey in the 1892 Buffalo, New York, crusade, tells his amazement of Moody's personal work, observing him lead the driver of a carriage to the Lord in the midst of a violent rainstorm.

In 1893 he had the "opportunity of the century." The World's Columbian Exposition (World's Fair) was to be held in Chicago from May 7 to October 31. He had a burden to saturate Chicago with the gospel during this time. Using many means and meetings in different languages, including 125 various Sunday services, thousands were saved. There were 1,933,210 who signed the guest register of the Bible School.

In 1895 he had a large crusade in Atlanta. That same year a roof collapsed on a crowd of 4,000 at Fort Worth, Texas. Fortunately, there were no deaths.

In 1897 he conducted another large Chicago crusade, packing out a 6,000 seat auditorium.

His church, which was renamed Moody Church in 1901, continued to progress with the following pastors: Erdman (1876-78), Charles M. Morton (1878-79), George C. Needham (1879-81), no regular pastor (1881-85),

Charles F. Goss (1885-90), Charles A. Blanchard (1891-93), and Reuben A. Torrey who began as pastor in 1894.

His interest in schools left him a lasting ministry. The forming of the Northfield Seminary (now Northfield School for Girls) in 1879, and the Mount Hermon Massachusetts School for Boys (1881) was the beginning. The Chicago Evangelization Society (later Moody Bible Institute) was opened with the first structure completed on September 26, 1889, with R. A. Torrey in charge. The school was an outgrowth of the 1887 Chicago Crusade.

In 1880 he started the famous Northfield Bible Conferences which continued until 1902, bringing some of the best speakers from both continents to the pulpit there. The world's first student conference was held in 1885 and the Student Volunteer Movement started two years later as a natural outgrowth.

In 1898 Moody was chairman of the evangelistic department of the Army and Navy Christian Commission of the Y.M.C.A. during the Spanish-American War.

He started his last crusade in Kansas City in November 1899. On November 16 he preached his last sermon on *Excuses* (Luke 14:16-24) and hundreds were won to Christ that night. He was very ill afterwards, the illness thought to be fatty degeneration of the heart. Arriving home in Northfield November 19 for rest, he climbed the stairs to his bedroom never to leave it again. He died about 7:00 a.m. December 22 with a note of victory. He is reported to have said such things as the following: "I see earth receding; heaven is approaching (or opening). God is calling me. This is my triumph. This is my coronation day. It is glorious. God is calling and I must go. Mama, you have been a good wife. . .no pain. . .no valley. . .it's bliss."

The funeral was on December 26 with C. I. Scofield, local Congregational pastor, in charge. Memorial services were held in many leading cities in America and Great Britain. Moody left to the world several books, although he never wrote a book himself. His Gospel sermons, Bible characters, devotional and doctrinal studies were all compiled from his spoken word, those after 1893 by A. P. Fitt. However, he read every article and book before they were published. His innumerable converts were estimated by some as high as 1,000,000.

R. A. Torrey, one of his closest friends, writes his conclusions in his famous *Why God Used D. L. Moody:* (1) fully surrendered, (2) man of prayer, (3) student of the Word of God, (4) humble man, (5) freedom from love of money, (6) consuming passion for the lost, (7) definite endument with power from on high.

Perhaps the world HAS seen what one man totally consecrated to God can do.

The Life
And Ministry Of

George Mueller
1805 ~ 1898

GEORGE MUELLER

BORN: September 27, 1805 **DIED:** March 10, 1898
Kroppenstaedt, Prussia (Germany) **Bristol, England**
LIFE SPAN: 92 years, 5 months, 11 days

George Mueller has proved to the world the truth of Philippians 4:19, and he will always be remembered as the man who got things from God. His testimony is an inspiration to Christians everywhere. Three weeks after his marriage, he and his wife decided to depend on God alone to supply their needs--never again to approach people about them. His salary was made up of pew-rents. Now he felt led to relinquish this completely. Wishing that all support be spontaneous, he put a box in the chapel for his needs; determining never to run into debt and to get his needs supplied only be requests to God Himself. This was October 1830. When he died in March 1998 sixty-eight years later, he had obtained from God more than anyone else who ever lived-- seven and a half million dollars.

Mueller was the son of Herr and Frau Mueller. His father was a Prussian tax collector. The family moved to Heimershleben, four miles away, in 1810. Soon two other sons were born. Strangely gullible, the father would entrust his small sons with considerable amounts of cash to teach them to acquire the habit of possessing money without spending it. This backfired, for George in particular devised numerous methods of using the money for himself without being detected. Before he was ten years old, he repeatedly stole from the government funds in his father's keeping.

Herr Mueller wanted his son to be a clergyman and make a good living in order to be able to support him when he became old. Schooling was obtained for George at Cathedral Classical School at Halberstadt with very little supervision given him from about age ten to sixteen. His mother died when he was 14. George was playing cards, not even aware of her illness that night. He spent the next day at a tavern with some friends.

Lutheran church confirmation classes started at this time, and it was a custom for candidates on the eve of confirmation to make a formal confession of their sins to the clergyman in the vestry. Mueller used the opportunity to cheat the clergyman of 11/12ths of the fee his father had given him for the cleric. Confirmed the Sunday after Easter 1820, he was now a religious lost person. When George was 15, his father was transferred to Schoenebeck, Prussia. The son was left at home to supervise some repairs and to study for the ministry. George was up to his old tricks. He collected money which the villagers owed his father for taxes, then took a trip whih he later called . . . "days of sin." He would stay in expensive hotels, sneaking out after a week without paying a bill. However, after a couple of weeks of this, he was caught and put in jail for 24 days. The elder Mueller bailed his son out; and soon George entered school at Nordhausen, Prussia, where he stayed for two and one half years. He studied from 4 a.m. until 10 p.m. The teacher said he had great promise but drinking and debauchery continued to cancel these acclaims.

This time (1820-1825) was also spent in contriving to provide himself with money for his bad habits.

In 1825, when 19 years old, he left school and entered Halle University as a student of Divinity. The University had 1,260 students, including some 900 divinity students preparing themselves for the Lutheran Church ministries. Here he decided he must reform if a parish was to ever choose him as pastor. He renewed an acquaintance in a tavern with a fellow student named Beta, who was a backslidden Christian. They were former school fellows. In August 1825 Mueller, Beta and two other students pawned some of their belongings to get enough money for a few days of travel. Switzerland was decided upon, and George forged the necessary letters from their parents with which to get passports. Mueller, like Judas, decided to carry the purse. His friends unwittingly paid part of his expenses as a result and 43 idle days of travel followed.

Back at the University, Beta was stricken with remorse and made full confession to his father. Beta began to attend a Saturday night Christian meeting in a home. Mueller, hearing about this, became sincerely interested and pressed his friend into taking him to the meeting. Beta did, reluctantly, not believing George would like it--reading the Bible, praying, singing hymns, and listening to a sermon. As he sat in the Wagner residence, George saw something he had never seen before--people on their knees praying. He felt awkward for being there and even apologized for his presence. The host pleasantly invited him to come as often as he pleased. As he walked home, he declared, "All we have seen on our journey to Switzerland and all our former pleasures are as nothing in comparison with this evening!" That Saturday night in mid-November 1825 turned him around as Christ became his Saviour. At age 20 the unstable pagan found the power to overcome his moral weaknesses and a new life began.

In January 1826, as he began reading missionary literature, he felt inclined in this direction more and more. He wrote his father and brother to this end. However, the reply from father was a furious objection to these plans. As a result, George decided he would have to support himself at the University rather than take funds from his father. Back at Halle he obtained a well-paying job of teaching German to American college professors and translating lectures for them. He preached his first sermon on August 27, 1826, at a village six miles from Halle. During this time he lived for two months in the orphan House built by August Hermann Francke, Professor of Divinity at Halle. Here the seed of an idea was sown that was to come to fruition later in Bristol. In 1828 he completed his University courses.

Mueller now had a desire to become a missionary to the Jews, so he applied to a society in London which majored in this work, which led to an invitation to come for a six-month probationary priod in London. He left home on February 10, 1829, and arrived in London on March 19. His English became fluent although he never lost his German accent. The regulations and routine at seminary tempted him to give up his ideas. His study of Hebrew was unremitting and soon resulted in delicate health. Advised by doctors and friends, he went to the country for a change or air and schedule which was to change his life as well. He traveled to Teignmouth in Devonshire and became acquainted with Henry Craik, who would become his loyalassociate in the ensuing years. Here he attended the reopening of a small meeting-house called Bethesda Chapel where he was touched deeply by one of the speakers. By the time he returned to London, he was a different man, having learned the value of meditation upon the Scriptures, beginning in August 1829.

Now he began to gather some of his fellow students from 6 to 8 each morning for prayer and Bible reading. Evenings he would pray with anyone he could find, often until after midnight. During these days he felt he did not want to be limited to ministry amongst the Jews alone so he resigned from the London Society. Back in the Devonshire area he began to preach in chapels in Exmouth, Teignmouth and Shaldon. He was then called upon to pastor at the Ebenezer Chapel in Teignmouth, a congregation of 18 people, where he began in 1820. During this year he became convinced of the necessity of believer's baptism and was rebaptized. In January of 1830 he undertook a monthly preaching engagement just outside Exeter, lodging there with a Mrs. Hake, an invalid. Mary Groves, age 29, was keeping house for her. Mueller, with a mature outlook on life, was greatly attracted to Mary, though he was only 24 years of age. On October 7, 1830, they were joined in marriage at St. David's Church in Exeter.

Three weeks after their marriage, they decided to depend upon God alone to provide their needs as already indicated. They carried it to the extent that they would not give definite answers to inquiries as to whether or not they were in need of money at any particular moment. At the time of need, there would always seem to be funds available from some source, both in regards to their private income and to the funds for his vast projects soon to be discussed. No matter how pressing was the need, George simply renewed his prayers and either money or food always came in time to save the situation. On February 19, 1832, he records an instance of healing by faith. Suffering from a gastric ulcer, he believed God could heal him and four days later he was as well as ever. In the spring of 1832 he felt he must leave Teignmouth. Craik, his friend, had gone on to Bristol for a visit, and Mueller felt led to go there also. On April 22 he preached his first sermon in Bristol. A friend offered to rent Bethesda Chapel there for a year if the two men would stay and develop a work. Agreeing not to be bound by any stipulation, Craik and Mueller accepted the call. On May 25, 1832, the Muellers settled permanently in Bristol which became his home until he died. A long association with the chapel on Great George Street also began. In July of that year, Bristol was visited with a plague of cholera which took many lives, but none of those among whom he and Craik ministered. On September 17, 1832, his first child Lydia was born.

It was on February 25, 1834, that George Mueller founded a new Missionary Institution which he called "The Scriptural Knowledge Institution for Home and Abroad." It had four objectives:

1. To assist Sunday Schools, Day Schools and Adult Schools

and, where possible, to start new ones.

2. To sell Bibles and Testaments to the poor at low prices and, if necessary, to give them free of cost.

3. To aid missionary effort. (This was to provide financial aid to free-lance missionaries).

4. To circulate tracts in English and in various foreign languages.

The Orphan House became a fifth objective and the most well known enterprise, yet is is right to point out that Mueller was greatly used in developing the other objectives as well.

On March 19, 1834, a son Elijah was born, but he died the next year, June 25, 1835, from pneumonia leaving the Muellers with only one child--Lydia. The summer of 1835 found Mueller himself in very poor health, slowing down his pace and giving him time to write *The Narrative of the Lord's Dealing with George Mueller.*

For some time he had been thinking about starting an orphanage in Bristol. On December 9, 1835, he presented his burden at a public meeting. No collection was taken but someone handed him ten shillings and a Christian woman offered herself for th work. After five days of prayer $300 came in and it seemed they might now have enough money to rent a house, equip and furnish it. The other request was for Christian people to work with the children. His basic aim was to have a work--something to point to as visible proof that God hears and answers prayer. His heart went out to the many ragged children running wild in the streets but that was a secondary reason for starting the orphanage.

He rented Number 6 Wilson Street where he himself had been living; and on April 11, 1836, the doors of the orphanage opened with 26 children. These were girls between seven and twelve years old. The second house was opened on November 28, 1836, to care for children from babyhood to seven years of age. In September 1837, a third house was opened for boys over seven years of age.

Illness plagued Mueller from time to time and in lat 1837 he was very weak. This time his head provided the discomfort. He went to Germany in the spring of 1838 as well as in February 1840, when he saw his father for a last time. Presumably he still had not accepted Christ as George noted, "How it would have cheered the separation on both sides were my dear father a believer." He died shortly thereafter. The years 1828 to 1843 were surely years of trials for Craik and Mueller as they prayed in everything. All were properly clad and everyone sat down to regular meals in the Houses. Mueller never incurred a debt, and God supernaturally provided for everyone. A well known story indicates the kind of life that was lived.

One morning the plates and cups and bowls on the table were empty. There was no food in the larder and no money to buy food. The children were standing waiting for their morning meal when Mueller said, "Children, you know we must be in time for school." Lifting his hand he said, "Dear Father, we thank Thee for what Thou art going to give us to eat." There was a knock on the door. The baker stood there and said, "Mr. Mueller, I couldn't sleep last night. Somehow I felt you didn't have bread for breakfast and the Lord wanted me to send you some. So I got up at 2 a.m. and baked some fresh bread and have brought it." Mueller thanked the man. No sooner had this transpire when there was a second knock at the door. It was the milkman. He announced that his milk cart had broken down right in front of the Orphanage, and he would like to give the children his cans of fresh milk so he could empty his wagon and repair it. No wonder, years later, when Mueller was to travel the world as an evangelist he would be heralded as "the man who gets things from God.!"

By March 1843, he felt the need for a second home for girls. On July 1844, the fourth house on Wilson Street was opened--the total of his homeless waifs now being 130. A letter received on October 30, 1845, changed his entire ministry. . .he was now age 40. Basically, it was a letter from a local resident complaining that the noise of the children was a nuisance. They were vastly over-crowded and there was not enough space for land cultivation, washing clothes, etc. He gave the letter much thought, listing the pros and cons. If he were to leave, he would have to build a structure to hold at least 300 orphans at a cost of $60,000. On his 36th day of prayer over the delemma, the first $6,000 came in for a building program. By June 1848, he received all of the $60,000 which he needed. He had begun to build the previous year on July 5, 1847, at a place called Ashley Downs as the bulk of the money had been sent in. Building Number 1 was opened in June 1849 and housed 300 children with staff sufficient to teach and care for them. It was a seven-acre site and finally cost about $90,000 as legal expenses, furnishings and land purchase brought the price up higher than anticipated. The old houses on Wilson Street emptied and everyone was now under one roof.

Mueller was becoming a well known Christian leader. He answered some 3,000 letters a year without a secretary. Besides his orphanages, the four other objectives of his Scriptural Knowledge Institution claimed his attention and he continued his pastoral work at Bethesda Chapel also.

In 1850 he felt the need for a second orphanage. Donations began to come in miraculously again; and finally, on November 12, 1857, a second building was built housing 400 children at a cost of $126,000. Number 3 opened on March 12, 1862, housing 450 children and costing over $138,000. It was housed on 11 1/2 acres. Number 4 was opened November 5, 1868, and Number 5 on January 6, 1870. These last two cost over $300,000 and housed 450 each.

From 1848 to 1874, money came in to improve and expand the work which went from 130 orphans to 2,050 during this time and up to 13 acres. Mueller describes these days, writing in 1874:

> But God, our infinite rich Treasurer, remains with us. It is this which gives me peace. Moreover if it pleases Him, with a work requiring about $264,000 a year. . .would I gladly pass through all these trials of faith with regard to means, if He only might be glorified, and His Church and the world benefited. . .I have placed myself in the position of

having no means at all left; and 2,100 persons, not only daily at the table, but with everything else to be provided for, and all the funds gone; 189 missionaries to be assisted, and nothing whatever left; about one hundred schools with 9,000 scholars in them, to be entirely supported, and no means for them in hand; about four million tracts and tens of thousands of copies of the Holy Scriptures yearly now to be sent out, and all the money expended. . .I commit the whole work to Him, and He will provide me with what I need, in future also, though I know not whence the means are to come.

His own personal income varied around $12,000 a year, of which he kept for himself $1,800 giving the rest away.

His fellow worker, Henry Craik, died on January 22, 1866, followed by the death of his wife on February 6, 1870. She was 72 and had suffered from rheumatic fever. James Wright married Mueller's daughter, Lydia, in 1871 and also replaced Craik as his associate. Mueller himself remarried on November 30, 1871, to a Susannah Grace Sangar, whom he had known for 25 years as a consistent Christian. He was 66 and she in her late forties, a perfect companion for him in his ministries still ahead.

Mueller decided to fulfill the many requests for his appearance around the world. Turning the work over to Wright, from 1875 to 1892, Mueller made 16 preaching trips to various sectors of the world. For the sake of historians and others interested in statistical data, they were as follows:

1. March 26 - July 6, 1875 England (Brighton, London, Sunderland, Newcastle). Preached 70 times, such places as Spurgeon's Metropolitan Tabernacle, etc.
2. August 14, 1875 - July 5, 1876, England, Scotland and Ireland. His five week stay in Liverpool had Sunday crowds of 5,000.
3. August 16, 1876 - June 25, 1877, Switzerland, Germany and Holland. Preached 302 times in 68 places in three languages.
4. August 18, 1877 - July 8, 1878, Canada and the United States. Preached 299 times, conference with President Rutherford Hayes.
5. September 5, 1878 - July 18, 1879, Switzerland, France, Spain, Italy. Fellowship with Spurgeon in France, saw schools he supported in Spain.
6. August 27, 1879 - June 17, 1880, United States and Canada. Spoke again 299 times - in 42 places.
7. August 23, 1881 - May 31, 1881, Canada and the United States. Accepted many invitations he had to turn down the previous tour.
8. August 23, 1881 - May 30, 1882, Egypt, Palestine, Syria, Asia Minor, Turkey, Greece. Many physical difficulties were encountered, traveling was primitive.
9. August 8, 1882 - June 1, 1882, Germany, Austria, Hungary, Bohemia, Russia, Poland. Suppressed in Russia, could only preach to 20 at one time.
10. September 26, 1883 - June 5, 1884, India. 78 years old, preached 206

times and travelled 21,000 miles.

11. August 18 - October 2, 1884, England and South Wales. Tour cut short because of illness of Mrs. Mueller.

12. May 16 - July 1, 1885, England Tour cut short because of illness of George Mueller.

13. September 1 - October 3, 1885, England and Scotland, Primary ministry was in Liverpool, England, and Dundee, Scotland.

14. November 4, 1885 - June 13, 1887, Australia, China, Japan, Straits of Malacca. Ages 81 - 83 - travelled 37,280 miles around the world.

15. August 10, 1887 - March 11, 1890, Australia, Tasmania, New Zealand, Ceylon, India. Intense heat of Calcutta almost killed him. Telegram that daughter Lydia had died January 10, 1890, in Bristol cut short the tour.

16. August 8, 1890 - May 1892, Germany, Switzerland, Austria, Italy. At 86 preaching to large crowds.

George and his wife travelled 200,000 miles in 17 years of world-wide evangelism efforts, in 42 countries, preaching to 3 million people.

It was on January 13, 1894, that his second wife passed away after 23 years of marriage. He was now 89 years old and was living out his days in Orphan House No. 3. He preached his last sermon on Isaiah's Vision, March 6, 1898, at Alma Road Chapel in Clifton. On March 10, 1898, the maid went to his room and found him dead on the floor by the side of his bed. The funeral in Bristol on March 14 has never been surpassed there as tens of thousands lined the streets. The grief of the orphans was evident. He was buried by the side of his two wives.

Mueller was non-sectarian in his general outlook and was one of the founders of the Brethren movement. His influence touched the lives of thousands --perhaps most notable that of J. Hudson Taylor. His most moving reunion with an orphan was on October 19, 1878, when a 71 year old widow met him. . .she had been his first orphan over 57 years previously. Ten thousand and twenty-five other orphans wre to follow her there and have Daddy Mueller rear them. Mueller read the Bible through over 200 times, half of these times on his knees. He said he knew of some 50,000 specific answers to prayer. . .requests to God alone!

Over 3,000 of his orphans were won to Christ by him.

The Life
And Ministry Of

John Richard Rice
1895 ~ 1980

JOHN RICHARD RICE

BORN: December 11, 1895   **DIED:** December 29, 1980
Gainesville, Texas   Murfreesboro, Tennessee
LIFE SPAN: 85 years, 18 days

John R. Rice has been one of the most widely used and controversial figures in Christendom. But none can deny his accomplishments. He revived the spirit of evangelism in America in the mid 20th Century when it had almost faded from the American scene, and he certainly has to be considered one of the most prolific writers in the history of the Christendom. His weapons have been the weekly *Sword of the Lord* for over 40 years. The conducting of soul-winning conferences has helped ignite the fires of soul-winning and evangelism in more preacher's bones than has any man of his time. Daring to be different, in preaching and convictions, Rice is one of the most under-rated Christian leaders of this century. In truth, he is one of the most significant men in Christian history.

He was born the son of Will and Sallie (LaPrade) Rice, the second of five children. Home was in the country outside Gainesville, Texas, where Will Rice pastored in a little building at a crossroads called Vilot Community. From early days his mother called John "her preacher boy," which was to be remarkable fulfilled in later years. In September 1901, when John was five, his mother died. He never forgot her plea for her children to meet her in Heaven. John attended the First Baptist Church of Gainesville. One Sunday morning the pastor, A. B. Ingram, preached on "The Prodigal Son." John, age nine, slipped to the front of the church to make public his profession of Christ. No one showed him any Scripture, so it was three years before he got assurance of his salvation by reading John 5:24.

The same year his father moved from Gainesville to Dundee, in West Texas, where he married Dolous Bellah. There John lived with his family until he went to Decatur College.

He won his first soul to Christ at age fifteen at a revival meting when a fourteen year old boy responded to the preaching by raising his hand. No public invitation was given, so Rice talked to him outside the building and led him to Christ.

John grew up in poverty conditions but learned how to get things from God. After finishing what high school courses were available, Rice decided to study for a teacher's examination. Upon receiving a teacher's certificate, he taught in a country school fifteen miles from his home, earning $220 for his four-month efforts. He felt an increasing burden to continue his schooling and broaden his education, so he began to pray much about this possibility.

In January 1916 he packed his clothes, saddled his cowpony and started off through the rain toward Decatur (Texas) Baptist College, some 125 miles away with about $9.35. He was able to borrow $60 from the bank in Archer City, Texas, and soon he was enrolled in school. He milked the college cows and later was asked to be one of the two waiters who served in the dining room. It was here he met Lloys McClure Cooke whom he would marry five years later.

One week after seeing the first football game in his life, he joined the college team as a regular tackle and played for the next two seasons. He was never knocked out or taken out from the moment he first began to play the game. He graduated in the spring of 1918.

Rice was then drafted into the army and sent to Camp Travis. He served in the Army for eight months where he was in the hospital with mumps and missed going overseas, so he went on guard duty and finally was assigned to the Dental Corps. He was discharged in January 1919 and immediately enrolled at Baylor University in Waco, Texas, from which he graduated with his A.B. degree in 1920 after only one and half years.

He worked his way through college, getting up at 5:20 every morning to deliver mail from Waco to the University. He then milked the Baylor cows, strained the milk and put it away, until it was time to dry the dishes in the girls' dormitory. In addition, he worked at the University bookstore and served as a janitor for a local Baptist church. This was all besides the mission Sunday school he conducted for the same church, plus his studies, which ultimately brought him the 1914 Class Scholarship. This scholarship was presented each year to some worthy student who, by good scholarship, leadership, and character deserved honor. The tremendous pace of Dr. Rice in later years can be attributed to his learning to work early in life.

He took a teaching position in English at Wayland Baptist College in Plainview, Texas, and also coached football and basketball teams there. In the spring of 1921 he attended the University of Chicago, looking forward to a master's degree in education and psychology.

One night he took off from his studies to attend services at the Pacific Garden Mission where Rev. Holland Oates addressed the men. He wasn't polished but the message surely touched Rice. If God could use this man, surely a college English teacher should be able to be used also. That night he knelt beside a drunken bum and led him to Christ. His life work now seemed to be altered. . .no longer political and educational goals, but he was determined to pursue the souls of men!

Soon he left the University of Chicago and returned to Texas where he led singing in revival meetings throughout the state in the summer of 1921. He borrowed $100 to get married on September 27, 1921, to Lloys McClure Cooke at her father's farmhome near Muenster, Texas.

Next he enrolled in Southwestern Baptist Theological Seminary at Fort Worth, Texas, in the fall of 1921 and stayed until the spring of 1923. During these days, he preached in jails, on street corners, and served as student pastor to rural churches in Cooke and Fannin counties. His summers were filled with revival campaigns. Upon leaving the seminary he became associate pastor of the First Baptist Church of Plainview where he stayed for a year. He then accepted the pastorate of the First Baptist Church of Shamrock, Texas, where from 1924 to 1926 the church grew from 200 to 460 members.

In 1926 John Rice moved to Fort Worth, Texas, to enter the field of evangelism. He became associated more and more with a great independent

Baptist there, J. Frank Norris, and often supplied the pulpit in Norris' absence. This relationship brought him enemies as well as friends. Opposition came from the Southern Baptists who insisted Rice break ties with Norris. This, plus Rice's opposition to some of the denomination's practices and teaching, began to close some of the Convention churches to him. However, his daily radio broadcast gave him many friends in Oklahoma and Texas.

Purchasing a tent, he held many good campaigns--beginning in the Fort Worth area. John then pitched his tent in Decatur, Texas, where his father lived. The revival lasted ten weeks resulting in many hundreds of conversions! Most of the churches had opposed his revival, so in order to care for the new converts, a tabernacle was erected and a new church began with 500 people. Then he went to Waxahachie, Texas, where he took a former livery stable and workers built seats for about 1,200. The twelve-week campaign ended with some 300 converts again organizing a new church. Then on to Sherman, Texas, where it happened again--1 weeks of revival and a new church organized with another 300 people. Other cities experienced much of the same kind of blessing. Before this phase of his life was over, he was to build eight tabernacles with five becoming permanent churches.

In July 1932 John Rice began an open air revival in Dallas. He had no money, no building, no organization--just God. Three weeks later, after hundreds had been saved, a group met on July 31 to organize the Fundamentalist Baptist Church of Oak Cliff. Nine hundred united with the work in a little under two years, and Rice stayed on to pastor until 1939. The membership grew to 1,700 with 8,000 professing salvation.

It was here that *The Sword of the Lord* was begun on September 28, 1934. The revival weekly had printed 5,000 copies its first issue and was offered for $1 per year subscription.

Norris in Fort Worth and Rice in Dallas were proving that independent Baptist churches could thrive in the midst of strong Southern Baptist Convention country. However, 1936 brought a tragic split between them. Rice felt that Norris, one of the world's great preachers, sometimes attacked good men without justification. This he opposed, especially a forthcoming article on Sam Morris, another pastor and radio preacher. In January of that year, Rice had scheduled a campaign in Binghamton, New York. Norris did all he could do to cancel this crusade. He warned the pastor that Rice was a Holy Roller, accusing him of preaching "McPhersonism and Pentecostalism." With many supportive letters in hand, the local pastor let the meetings proceed; they soon outgrew his Grace Baptist Church. Services moved to the Binhamton Theater seating 2,200 and several other churches joined in the revival series. From January 12 to February 23, Rice preached with some 374 public conversions recorded. The January 31 issue of Norris's *Fundamentalist* described the "Rice heresy" as "one of the outstanding heresies of modern times;" whereas the February 6 issue of *The Sword of the Lord* had Rice urging people to forgive Norris for his charges and to support him.

A tragedy of a somewhat different nature took place on November 23, 1938, when his church in Dallas burned down. Fire was seen suddenly shooting up above the baptistery while a missionary named Skivington from South America was speaking. The church building was a total loss without one cent of insurance on the property. Starting all over again, the church recovered and on December 22, 1939, the name of the church was changed to the Galilean Baptist Church.

It was on January 19, 1940, that *The Sword of the Lord* announced Rice's resignation from the pastorate to enter the field of full-time evangelism. The year 1939 had found Rice in various sections of the country --and now the fires of evangelism were burning in his bones. It was a time when city-wide campaigns and mass evangelism had all but disappeared. Bob Jones, Sr., and Mordecai Ham were finishing up great careers, but there was nobody new on the horizon, with the exception of Hyman Appelman. Rice was proud of the title "evangelist" even though the name generally was not too well thought of at that time. *The Sword of the Lord* was having an impact. Great soul winners of the past and their messages were featured. Such things as evangelism, preaching against sin, the public invitation, the evangelistic church, and the fullness of the Spirit were promoted. It was Rice who was leading the way into a new generation of revival and evangelism, winning thousands of souls along the way. The spring of 1940 found Rice moving his family, the paper, the office, and the bookstore from Dallas to Wheaton, Illinois. One reason for this move was his desire to get his six daughters under the influence of Wheaton College.

Praying one morning in a YMCA room on the south side of Chicago, Rice pledged himself to God to bring back mass evangelism to America. Having majored in single church campaigns, he was now getting invitations from groups of pastors to have him lead them in union campaigns. One of the first such campaigns was in Minneapolis where sixteen churches chaired by Richard Clearwaters called Rice. . .some 200 were saved. In March 1944, it was Everett, Washington, with Stratton Shufelt as his regular songleader and soloist, some 300 to 400 were saved. In April 1944, he held one of his largest campaigns in Buffalo, New York, at the Kleinhans Music Hall. Closing services saw thousands crowd in with hundreds standing or turned away. Some 115 churches participated and the number of first-time decisions was 997. Another great campaign was in Cleveland, Ohio, February 11 to March 11, 1945, with 93 cooperating churches. This campaign had some 800 first-time decisions for Christ and a closing night crowd of 3,767 jamming the Cleveland Public Music Hall. Again Shufelt was heading a fine musical program. Rice was now 49 years old. Youth for Christ and Jack Wyrtzen were a new phenomenon, and evangelism was becoming popular again. Hundreds of young men were entering the field of evangelism, many from Bob Jones University. Rice continued to do the work of two men for several years --large scale evangelism and editing and writing. In January of 1946, some 48 churches sponsored him in Pontiac, Michigan. In March 1946, it was Miami, Florida, where 44 Baptist churches sponsored him, and in fifteen days there were 600 professions of faith at the meetings and another 400 in the public school meetings. A great Chicago crusade was held in May of 1946 with Rice speaking during the final fifteen days. . .the first united campaign there since Sunday's meetings in 1918. Over 2,000 decisions were made during the series which also featured Bob Jones, Sr., and Paul Rood in the weeks preceding Rice's ministry. In September 1946, Rice held a campaign in Dayton, Ohio, with some 500 decisions for Christ at the meetings and 450 more at the high school services. Harry D. Clarke was now his songleader. In January 1947, twenty churches brought him to Lima, Ohio, with some 500 saved at services and schools. The Rice-Clarke team was in Marion, Ohio, in February with over 200 first-time professions of faith. In March and April, the team held a large tent campaign in San Pedro, California, with some 600 decisions for Christ. Seattle, Washington, Winston -Salem, North Carolina, and other cities were also to be stirred.

The Sword of the Lord was growing by leaps and bounds as well, and soon Rice had to decide where to spend the bulk of his time, as an editor, trying to influence Christians weekly in revival emphasis, or as an evangelist in crusades across the country. Both would contribute to the winning of the lost. But after much consideration, the nod was given to *The Sword of the Lord.* Other evangelists on the scene could perpetuate the mass crusades that Rice and Appelman gave birth to in the early 1940's.

With purpose never wavering in 41 years of issues, the weekly masthead continues to read, "An Independent Christian Weekly, Standing for the Verbal Inspiration of the Bible, the Deity of Christ, His Blood Atonement, Salvation by Faith, New Testament Soul Winning and the Premillennial Return of Christ. Opposes Modernism, Worldliness and Formalism." The paper averaged 7,200 copies weekly the first year--1934. It reached 100,000 weekly in 1955; and some 200,000 in 1972; and then 300,000 in 1975 making it the largest independent religious weekly in the world. It is published with Portuguese and Spanish editions as well. There has probably never been a periodical in history that has seen so many saved and so many Christians challenged to revival and soulwinning.

When Dr. Rice moved to Wheaton, the office work was done in his home. In 1945, a basement office was rented in the business section of Wheaton. In 1946, a large, two story brick warehouse was purchased and remodeled. In 1952 another two story brick building was purchased and in 1955 the First Presbyterian Church property was purchased to provide location for future building. Sword of the Lord Foundation was incorporated as a non-profit organization in 1947.

John Rice's evangelistic campaigns were replaced by periodic conferences on revival and soulwinning held at conference grounds and in strategic churches. This has continued through the years, stirring the fires of revival in thousands of Christians' lives. In recent years, Jack Hyles has become his co-worker in this ministry. The first of these conferences were held at the Bethany Reformed Church in Chicago. In 1945 a large conference was conducted at Winona Lake, Indiana. Six evangelists agreed to work toward nationwide revival campaigns: John Rice, Bob Jones, Sr., Hyman Appelman, Jesse Hendley, Robert Wells, and Joe Henry Hankins. Repeat conferences were held in 1946 and 1947. After 1947, ironically, they were notified that they were not welcome back to the grounds housing the late Billy Sunday's activities, (a man he was trying to follow.) Under new leadership, however, they were back in 1976. National conferences of great magnitude were held in Indianapolis in 1974, in Dallas in 1975 and Atlanta in 1976.

Rice's book sales have been phenomenal, beginning with the tract/booklet, *"What Must I do to be Saved?"* written in San Antonio, Texas, during a revival campaign in the late 1920's, and first published in *The Fundamentalist,* Norris's paper. Some 15 million copies have been distributed and thousands of souls have been saved. It is in some 38 different languages. Along with Ford Porter's famous tract, *God's Simple Plan of Salvation,* and Campus Crusades *God's Four Spiritual Laws,* it is one of the most effective and widely used explanations of salvation's plan in print today. His first sermon was put into print in 1931.

Soon he was compiling his sermons into booklets and books, and writing on specific issues such as lodges, the movies, woman's attire, prayer, the Holy Spirit, etc. In 1967 Moody Press published a list of over 10,000 books in print from 57 religious publishing companies. The one man who was responsible for the most books/booklets published was Rice, with some 142 different titles and/or editions, more than doubling the second place entry, Harry Ironside, who had 65. The titles, too numerous to mention, are widely accepted by Christians everywhere. In 1936 his first clothbound book came out entitled, *The Coming Kingdom of Christ.* His book, *Prayer, Asking and Receiving* (1942), sold 250,000 copies in these years, besides 8 foreign language editions. *The Power of Pentecost* is considered a classic on the Holy Spirit. His booklet, *What is Wrong With the Movies?* has caused thousands of people to turn away from movie attendance for more consecrated lives. *The Soul Winner's Fire,* published by Moody Press, was another outstanding booklet. In 1973 the tally was 134 titles with a circulation of 47 million in over 38 different languages.

Rice stayed on in Wheaton until 1963, when he moved most of his large staff to Murfreesboro, Tennessee. While in Wheaton, he founded the Calvary Baptist Church. Rice has six children, all daughters, and they all married men active in the Lord's work. Grace was the first, born October 22, 1922. Along came Mary Lloys (June 27, 1925), Elizabeth (May 18, 1927), Jessie (January 13, 1929), Joanna (November 3, 1931), and finally Joy (September 27, 1937). Allan MacMullen, Charles Himes, Walt Handford, Don Sandberg, William Carl Rice and Roger Martin, the husbands, all have made valuable contributions to the work of the Lord.

Rice has been engaged in several controversies, two of note in recent years: The Chafer book, and the policies of Billy Graham since 1957. In the 1940's a book by Lewis S. Chafer entitled, *True Evangelism,* was produced by Moody Press. Feeling it to be a harmful book to the cause of evangelism, Rice protested loud and long about its continual promotion. In the 1950's, Rice was one of the first men along with Bob Jones, Sr. to take the unpopular position of opposing the sponsorship of Billy Graham's ecumenical crusades which began with the New York crusade of 1957. Previous to this, Rice had given Graham much encouragement by his reports of Graham's ministry in *The Sword*. It has never been a personal vendetta, but a matter of following his scriptural convictions.

Almost overlooked in his ministries is the fact that he is a radio preacher and a song writer. His *Voice of Revival* broadcast continues on more than 30 stations across the country. On one occasion years ago, he received 17,000 letters in one week resulting from his broadcast in the Philadelphia area. His songs such as *Never Lonely, Never Fearing, His Yoke is Easy, Souls are Dying, Oh, Bring Your Loved Ones, So Little Time, Jesus is Coming, The Price of Revival, We'll Never Say Goodbye, When Jesus Comes to Reign* have been a blessing to many.

His exciting story is told in depth in *Man Sent From God*, authored by Robert Sumner.

One of his final projects was the editing of *The Rice Reference Bible*, with his notes of a lifetime.

He preached his last message in Wadsworth, Ohio. Failing health overtook him and he soon passed on to his eternal home.

The Life
And Ministry Of

William Bell Riley
1861 ~ 1947

WILLIAM BELL RILEY

BORN: March 22, 1861
Green County, Indiana

DIED: December 5, 1947
Minneapolis, Minnesota

LIFE SPAN: 86 years, 8 months, 13 days

Riley was one of the most diligent fundamentalists of his day. For 45 years he was the pastor of the First Baptist Church of Minneapolis, Minnesota. Along with Norris in the South and Shields in Canada, Riley was the voice of historic Christianity against the infiltration of liberalism. His chief foes were the Northern (now American) Baptist Convention and evolution. Although he stayed to fight from within the denomination, never withdrawing his church, his stand will never be forgotten. William Bell Riley is known as "The Grand Old Man of Fundamentalism," and his accomplishments leave one breathless.

Born thirty days before the outbreak of the Civil War, he was reared in a Boone County, Kentucky, log cabin where his family had moved. Son of Branson and Ruth, he did his share of the chores. At age nine he frequently plowed and worked the fields from 5 a.m. to 9 p.m. In 1872 the family moved to Owen County, Kentucky, purchasing a 120 acre farm. He attended a country school at Union. His irregular attendance was due to the farm work which at times kept him home days at a time.

In August 1878, when he was seventeen, he made a public profession of his faith in Christ at the Baptist Church in Dallasburg, Kentucky, which was two and a half miles from his farm home and was baptized in a pond.

Riley earned a reputation as a debater in the public schools and was torn between a legal profession and a call to preach. After some months of turmoil, he knelt between two rows of tobacco on a hillside and said, "Lord, I give over, I give up, I will preach." He recalls that this was his greatest experience with God. At eighteen he rented his own farm and met his first real test in life. Walking out on a field of 24 acres of tobacco early one Sunday morning, he found that half the plants lay dead from the work of cut worms. Lying down in the open field, he wept. But the next day a heavy rain made it possible to replace most of the crop and in the next two years he paid off his bills and had a balance remaining.

With this money he went to a Normal School in Valparaiso, Indiana, the winter of 1879-80. Homesickness and financial difficulties were part of the agenda, but he received a teacher's certificate. An additional year was spent at home due to family difficulties, but in the fall of 1881 he was off to college. William decided upon a Presbyterian school, Hanover (Indiana) College, because of its spiritual reputation. He seriously pursued his new calling, majoring in the classics as well as being an active debater. He graduated with an A.B. degree in 1885 and received his M.A. degree in 1888. His father died while he was in college but was greatly pleased to know his son was called to preach. Riley started as a once-a-month preacher from 1881 to 1883 supplying in North Madison, Indiana. In 1883 he was made pastor of his own churches at Carrolton and Warsaw, Kentucky, preaching two Sundays a month in each place. Riley was ordained a Baptist minister on December 25, 1883, at

94

Dallasburg.

Riley completed his education at Southern Baptist Seminary in Louisville, Kentucky, graduating in 1888. While here he had a student pastorate at the Tabernacle Baptist Church of New Albany, Indiana 1887-88. In 1887, D. L. Moody held a campaign in Louisville and Riley was one of the personal workers. In June 1888 Riley gave his Seminary graduating address in the Broadway Baptist Church of Louisville on the subject "The Triumph of Orthodoxy."

That same month he was installed as pastor of the First Baptist Church of Lafayette, Indiana, which he pastored until 1890. He was instrumental in bringing Moody to town for a union campaign. It was here he met and fell in love with Lillian Howard and six weeks after their marriage on December 31, 1890, he baptized his young bride into the Baptist congregation as she had been a member of a local Methodist church. They were the parents of six children: Arthur (December 2, 1892), Mason (March 16, 1894), Herbert (1895. . .killed in a hunting accident at age 19), Eunice (October 14, 1902), William (November 29, 1904), and John (December 26, 1906).

In mid 1890 he accepted the pastorate of the First Baptist Church of Bloomington, Indiana, which he served until early 1893. Here, because of his protest against gambling, some 250 convictions were secured. He took the gamblers' written threats to the newspapers and defiantly published them, daring the senders to lay a hand on him.

Next, a new work, the Calvary Baptist Church of Chicago, called him. There were sixty members, a mission work of the First Baptist Church. By the time he left in 1897, the church had grown to about 500. Here his first determined fight against liberalism began. His frequent contacts with the professors of the University of Chicago soon gained him the reputation of being hopelessly orthodox. During the Chicago World's Fair in 1893, corruption and lawlessness mushroomed in spite of the efforts of D. L. Moody in his campaign for souls during those days. Riley and others joined the fight and kept some of the saloons closed on Sundays. Again he was threatened and this time he read the threats from the pulpit charging "criminality is cowardice" assuring his congregation there was no danger. During these days he often spoke for Billy Sunday at his noon-day meetings in a Chicago, Y.M.C.A., where the latter was the religious director.

A period of depression followed and money was very tight. The pastoral work became very difficult because of the severe living conditions of many. Riley gave so much time to visitation and aid in the daytime that his studying had to be done late at night. The church decided to merge with a Presbyterian and Christian congregation to pool their resources.

Now Riley began to pray for a smaller town to minister where he could influence a whole area for God as he felt he couldn't touch the entire city of Chicago. A confessed liberal, Dr. Charles Henderson, of the University of Chicago recommended him to the pulpit of the First Baptist Church of Minneapolis because he was unable to fill an invitation. Riley preached there in January of 1896. When he got off the train to candidate, he forgot one of his grips--the one containing the suit he was to wear. He had to preach that morning in an old sack suit which was not taken very well by the aristocracy of the church! After hearing about 25 other candidates, Riley was called there and began his ministry on March 1, 1897. The church roll was revised and cut down to 585 members. Then the church began to really grow. This growth was disturbing to certain elements in the church. Riley decided that certain things had to be changed and set out to accomplish them. Stormy sessions arose as young Riley proposed to discontinue pew rent, church "fairs" and money-raising suppers. Some members left, but the church prospered and became the denomination's largest with thousands of converts baptized there. Soon he was in the midst of civic reforms also. . .demanding adequate law enforcement of liquor laws. Riley's ministry was one of preaching the gospel as well as fighting foes of the gospel, and he was sympathetic and helpfully related to united evangelism helping R. A. Torrey and Gypsy Smith. He was chosen secretary to prepare for J. Wilbur Chapman's campaign in Minneapolis.

Riley's influence grew steadily across the country in four ways: his addresses delivered at metropolitan centers across the land; a series of debates involving most of the outstanding advocates of evolution; his writing. . .numerous books, newspaper, and magazine articles; and by the lives of his students from Northwestern Schools.

His addresses were given, for the most part, in connection with the founding of the World's Christian Fundamentalist Association which he was used to bring into existence. The aim of this movement was to declare war on Modernism. In 1918 Riley and A.C. Dixon asked six biblicists to meet them at R. A. Torrey's summer home to consider the possibilities of organizing disturbed evangelicals into a world-fellowship. A day of prayer and discussion started a foundation for the new group. Riley called for a meeting in Philadelphia on May 25, 1919, and 6,000 gathered, due for the most part to the labors of J. D. Adams of Philadelphia. Riley gave the opening and closing addresses and was elected President. The meetings continued through June 1. Nine points were drafted into a Confession of Faith with R. A. Torrey's mind dominating the final draft. The planks in essence included: 1. Scriptures verbally inspired. 2. One God existing in three persons. 3. Jesus Christ born of the Virgin Mary being true God and true man. 4. Sinfulness of mankind. 5. Christ dying for our sins. 6. Resurrection and High Priesthood of Christ. 7. Blessed Hope, personal pre-millennial and imminent return of Christ. 8. All who receive by faith the Lord Jesus become children of God. 9. Bodily resurrection of the just and unjust, and resulting everlasting blessedness of the saved and punishment of the lost. The word Fundamentalist came out of this conference. Lyman Stewart, found of B.I.O.L.A. in Los Angeles, offered $300,000 for the publication of a series of volumes on *The Fundamentals.* Nearly 3 million copies of these volumes went out to laymen, ministers and missionary workers around the world. Conferences in major cities followed and the movement went overseas as well. Annual conventions, confined for the most part to the United States and Canada, drew great speakers and great crowds.

Riley resigned as president in 1929 and the movement was led by Sidney Smith for two years followed by Paul Rood for many years. Riley later served as executive secretary.

William Bell Riley's addresses across the country were not only on defending the faith, but he also excelled as an evangelist, holding many city-wide campaigns with thousands being converted. In February 1912, a great crusade was held in Duluth, Minnesota, with between 500 to 1,000 converts. In Peoria, Illinois, a three week crusade was held in the City Armory and in Seattle, Washington, a tabernacle was built for a month's campaign, with many saved. In Dayton, Ohio, 66 churches constructed a tabernacle seating 5,000 and after a four week meeting, some 1,200 were added to their memberships. In 1933, at Worcester, Massachusetts, some 25 churches participated with 400 professions of faith.

He also held individual church campaigns, a notable one being at the First Baptist Church of Fort Worth, Texas. Three hundred fifty two were converted in the twelve day crusade.

Nor was he confined to America--his overseas ministries started in 191 when he went to England in response to the invitation of A. C. Dixon, the pastor of Spurgeon's Metropolitan Tabernacle. One Sunday there he saw some 60 people accept Christ. He spent four weeks there and another four weeks in other cities in England and Scotland. In 1929, in response to a call from the Bible League of England, Riley brought his wife and ministered in England, Scotland, Ireland, Belgium, and France. In 1936 he returned, this time sponsored by the Advent and Preparation Movement. He preached one week in Wales, one in Scotland, two in Ireland, a month in England and a week in Belgium and France.

The teachings of evolution was a hot issue in those days so his debates became another phase of his ministry. His first encounter was in Raleigh, North Carolina, when six professors from the State College who believed in evolution attacked the message of J. C. Massee at a Bible Conference there. He met a Professor Metcalf; and although no decision was rendered, debating (in which he had excelled in high school) was back in his blood. William Jennings Bryan had died in 1925 and the mantle for fighting evolution passed to Riley. Bryan had referred to Riley as "The greatest Christian statesman in the American pulpit." Riley's next debate in 1925 was scheduled for the Church of the Open Door in Los Angeles. At the last moment the antagonist backed out, conceding defeat leaving the building filled with 4,000 who were eager to view the proceedings. He led in a campaign against the exclusive teachings of evolution and Darwinism in 1926 at the University of Minnesota. His debates there opened a series of contests across the country between Riley and the leading evolutionists.

Maynard Shipley, president of the Science League of America, agreed to four debates with Riley. Riley won the first two by a ten to one margin and a substitute, Edward Cantrell, was engaged for the last two in the place of Shipley. He was field secretary for the Civil Liberties Union of America. The debates all went against Dr. Cantrell. He was easier yet to defeat, the Chicago vote being 1800 votes to twelve. Then Dr. Birkenhead, Unitarian pastor from Kansas City went down in three overwhelming defeats. Finally in desperation, the evolutionists imported from England Professor J. B. McCabe, author of many rationalistic books and ardent advocate of the evolutionary hypothesis. The first debate was about a tie, but the next three Riley won handily. In Toronto, he met McCabe again and now won ten to one. Riley took on McCabe in New York before a crowd of rationalists and atheists, but the verdict was seventeen to twelve in favor of Riley! After defeating Charles Smith, President of the American Association for the Advancement of Atheism, and Henry Holmes, Philosophy Department head of Swarthmore (Pennsylvania) College, it was hard to find opponents. Clarence Darrow was challenged several times, but he refused to meet Riley.

William Bell Riley's influence was felt also through his writings. He was responsible for some 90 books and many pamphlets and was renown for his fearless literature as well as his fearless preaching. His book, *The Menace of Modernism*, expresses his deep-seated contempt for university professors who slander the Bible. However, on a personal basis he sought to maintain a friendly spirit to the enemies of the faith and always acted as a true Christian gentleman.

In July 1923, Riley started on a colossal task of taking his church through the entire Bible in consecutive Lord's day studies. He did just that, completing this project ten years later on July 1, 1933. These sermons were published in forty volumes under the title *The Bible of the Expositor and the Evangelist.* This work is an exposition of the text and of the special use of certain portions of scripture in soul-winning appeals. *The Perennial Revival* (1933) was also widely received as was *The Preacher and His Preachings,* written just before he died. Other books include such titles as : *Revival Sermons; Wives of the Bible; My Bible, an Apologetic; Seven New Testament Soul Winners; Seven New Testament Converts; Conflict of Christianity With Its Counterfeits; Rethinking the Church; The Problems of Youth; The Philosophies of Father Coughlin; Pastor Problems; Saved or Lost; Is Jesus Coming Again?* Nearly one million of his books have been circulated. His own personal library consisted of some 3,000 volumes.

His work as an educator also endeared him to the Christian public. It was back in 1902 that seven laymen came to him requesting additional instruction in the Bible so that they could preach in nearby closed churches. On October 2 he called together representatives of several denominations and with their cooperation organized the Northwestern Bible School. The seven original students grew in number until it became the second largest Bible School in the world at the time of Riley's death, with some 1,200 students enrolled. The Seminary (opened October 5, 1935) with 47 students), and College (1943) were organized in later years.

In 1938 a recap was given covering the first 35 years of existence, student numbers had grown from seven to 815; teachers from two to 24; from no property to four beautiful buildings; from no money to an $84,000 expense account. Riley never took a cent of salary; but, on the contrary, was a constant contributor to its current expense. Riley edited *School and Church* 1916-20 & *The Northwestern Pilot* 1920-53.

Riley also found time to found the Anti-Evolution League with three others in 1923. Also, the Baptist Bible Union started in May 1923 in Kansas City meeting in a tent rented from Walter L. Wilson. Some 3,300 were present with T. T. Shields being elected president. O. W. VanOsdel asked Riley to lead a separatist group out of the Northern Baptists, but Riley turned him down about 1927.

One would wonder how a man could find time to do all of that which has been described and yet have time left to pastor his church. Well, pastor he did--and most successfully! The visit of Louis Entminger in 1920 revitalized the Sunday School resulting in the dedication of Jackson Hall--a $350,000 educational building on April 15, 1923.

Work was begun on a new 2,634 seat auditorium for his church which was dedicated on January 6, 1925. It was usually packed out, especially when he preached on evolution or modernism. The two buildings and property had a value of one million dollars. The missionary budget and membership at the church continued to increase also. He baptized 4,000 into the church and received another 3,000 by letter. It must be remembered that Minnesota is not Baptist country as Lutherans, Catholics, and Methodist dominate the population. There were only 35,000 Baptist church members in Minnesota during his days and he had one-tenth of them in his church.

His position in his denomination was a unique one. As stated, he never withdrew his church from the Convention, but it is believed that he did more than anyone else in slowing down the takeover by the liberals. He opposed the apostasy but he was unable to reverse the trend. Riley, as an individual, did withdraw from the Convention shortly before his death.

Horses, dogs and fishing were avid hobbies. All his life Riley was healthy and strong except for an eight month bout with insomnia in 1911 and in 1925 when he had a serious illness which threatened to take his life. Upon recovering from this, he preached the funeral of Charles Blanchard, fundamentalist president of Wheaton College in early 1926.

Riley's wife died on August 10, 1931 following surgery eight days previously. He was later married to Marie R. Acomb on September 1, 1933.

He retired from the church in 1942, becoming pastor emeritus, and devoted his remaining years to his schools. He became president of the Minnesota Baptist State Convention 1944-45. The phenomena of Youth for Christ was sweeping the nation and Riley became an ardent booster.

On March 22, 1946, he was honored on his 86th birthday at a civic luncheon at the Radisson Hotel. Present were Governor Luther W. Youndahl, Mayor Hubert H. Humphrey and speaker Dr. John E. Brown of Siloan Springs, Arkansas.

The following day, Sunday, March 23, the cornerstone of Memorial Hall, the new administration building of the Northwestern Schools, was laid. Riley hoped to raise one million dollars for a new set of buildings and saw the dynamic young Billy Graham as the man that could do it. So Graham was asked to succeed him as president upon Riley's death. He had also hoped Graham would use his influence to get the schools accredited. Graham headed the schools until 1952.

Shortly before midnight on December 5, 1947, William turned on his sick bed to say, "Goodbye, dear," to his wife at their home in Golden Valley, Minneapolis. . .and he was gone. Billy Graham conducted the funeral services. Riley's close friend and associate, Robert L. Moyer, was called to succeed him at the church but Moyer's untimely death in 1944 was a chock to all. An assistant pastor, Curtis B. Akenson, became pastor. The church has continued to belong to the Convention despite all the warnings along the way.

Northwestern Seminary was discontinued in 1956. The Bible School program was also phased out. Soon the College was out of business. It was reopened in the fall of 1972.

Riley also helped to popularize the daily vacation Bible school movement and was one of the early pioneers in it. One summer he sent 403 of his student body into this work. He was the editor of *The Christian Fundamentalist* from 1927 to 1932.

The Life
And Ministry Of

Lester Roloff
1914 ~ 1982

LESTER ROLOFF

BORN: June 28, 1914   **DIED:** November 2, 1982
Dawson, Texas   Texas
LIFE SPAN: 68 years, 4 months, 4 days

Lester Roloff was a perfect example of a modern day prophet. In all his years of serving God, he set the example for all who believe, man ought to obey God rather than men. Roloff was constantly engaged in battle against some of the forces of the state of Texas, primarily the Welfare Department-- they would silence or greatly curtail his ministry if they could. The irony of it all is that he had done nothing but help change lives of countless youngsters who had nobody else to help them. It is hard to believe that the story you are now going to read could happen in America.

Roloff was born on a farm ten miles south of Dawson, Texas, to Christian parents. He was saved in a little country church called Shiloh Baptist when about twelve in a revival in July 1926 under the ministry of John T. Taylor. High School was completed in Dawson. Reared on a farm, he took his milk cow and went off to Baylor University in 1933 and milked his way through college. He graduated in 1937 with a A.B. degree.

While at Baylor he was far from idle. He started pastoring among the Southern Baptists in a succession of pastorates. First was the Prairie Grove Mills Baptist Church in Navarro County where he had 67 converted in a revival to begin things. He also preached at his hometown church at Shiloh which was located outside of Dawson. Then he preached a revival at the First Baptist Church of Purden, Texas, and had 143 additions baptizing some 100 of them. This led to his call there while he retained the ministry at Navarro Mills. This latest venture happened his last year in college.

Roloff went on to Southwestern Seminary in Fort Worth for three years, 1937 to 1940, while he maintained his ministry at Purden, going then to the First Baptist Church of Trinidad, Texas, his last year in Seminary.

He married Marie Brady on August 10, 1936, at the First Baptist Church of Galveston, Texas. They had two daughters, Elizabeth (born June 20, 1937) and Pamela Kay, an adopted daughter.

From 1941 to 1944 he pastored the Magnolia Park Baptist Church in Houston, Texas, which had great crowds and much blessing. He was president of the local pastors' conference during some of this time.

In 1944 he went to Corpus Christi where he remained the rest of his life. The Park Avenue Baptist Church extended a call to him where he went in March. On October 15, 1944, the church burned and later property was purchased in another location of town and the church became known as the Second Baptist Church which he pastored from 1944 to 1951 with some 3,300 additions during this time. A branch mission church was started called the West Heights Baptist Church.

Roloff began a radio ministry on May 8, 1944, with his Family Altar Program, first broadcast over a 250-watt station locally. Soon it was on more than 22 stations, approximately 65 hours a week, gradually increasing to 150 stations. Some of the broadcasts were 15 minutes in length, some one-half hour. Starting on the small KEYS station it had an interesting history. He was kicked off the radio ten months after he started; his fight against liquor being a prime reason. The next day he started to broadcast on KWBU, a 50,000-watt station where he held forth for eight years. In 1954 they decided to remove him because he was a controversial figure. Some businessmen bought the station and he was again on the air for a year. Then total programming conveniently removed him. The owners then lot $70,000 in one year. Roloff decided to try and buy the station and asked how much they wanted. The answer was $300,000 and he did not have a dime. However, with the help of God and the money of friends, $25,000 was put down as earnest money with $100,000 needed 90 days later. He had it all but $7,250 on the last day and $250 the last hour, but 45 minutes before the 2 p.m. deadline, it was all there! Others, of course, became stockholders and owned the station, but Roloff was the vehicle used to get it (called KCIA) in the right hands.

Roloff founded the Park Avenue Christian Day School in 1946. The school operated a kindergarten and continued through upper grades. His headquarters continued at the Park Avenue Day School, located on the property of the former Park Avenue Church.

In April 1951 he resigned as pastor of Second Baptist Church to enter full time evangelism. He found the Roloff Evangelistic Enterprises, a non-profit organization which sponsored many projects of faith. In May 1955 he printed his first issue of *Faith Enterprise,* a quarterly publication dedicated to the salvation of lost souls and strengthening believers.

In August of 1954, with convictions about being independent, he founded a church in Corpus Christi which was to be called the Alameda Baptist Church. He and four others put up $2,500 on ten and four-tenths acres of ground, and it was organized with 126 members on October 24. He pastored there until about 1961.

On March 13, 1956, Roloff stood in Waco Hall in Waco, Texas, and spoke to more than 2,000 giving his swan song to Baylor University. He stated all the issues in no uncertain terms.

Other ministries soon developed. Roloff described at least six major ministries that he was responsible for...

> Thirty years ago we started the Good Samaritan Rescue Mission that is still in operation. More than twenty years ago, the CITY OF REFUGE was started in an old Quonset hut given by Dr. Logan and put together by alcoholics at Lexington, Texas. The City of Refuge is now located in Culloden, Georgia, on 273 acres of an old antebellum home with lovely dormitories for men and women.

> The LIGHTHOUSE houseboat was built by Brother E. A. Goodman and taken down the Intracoastal Canal in 1958. On the way down, a boy fell off and went under this boat and missed the propeller. He was rescued by an unsaved boys who was going down to the Lighthouse for help and one of

our preacher boys, Bob Smith, who is now a missionary. This is where Bill Henderson, Ricky Banning and many others found God's will for their lives. We have preacher boys that have come to the Lighthouse to study for the ministry in other Christian schools. I have just dwelt with three eighteen year old boys in Corpus Christi within the last week who are drug addicts. The Lighthouse is located forty miles down the Intracoastal Canal from Corpus Christi and it can only be reached by plane or by boat.

The PEACEFUL VALLEY HOME for our older retired Christian friends is the prayer place. It is located near Mission and Edinburg, Texas, with many acres of citrus fruit and lovely vegetables that are grown there, in the midst of a lot of nice weather. This home is just for Christians who want to retire in a lovely place and still be of service to others. It began in 1969.

The ANCHOR HOME FOR BOYS with three big two-story buildings for dormitories, a cafeteria, gymnasium, shop building and dining room, is located at Zapata, Texas. It has a capacity for nearly three hundred boys.

The BETHESDA HOME FOR GIRLS in Hattiesburg, Mississippi, is for girls in trouble. It is a very beautiful home, located on Blue Lake, for both pregnant and delinquent girls. It has made many friends and received a warm welcome in Mississippi.

The REBEKAH HOME FOR GIRLS, located in Corpus Christi, Texas, is our largest home. We have had fifteen hundred girls in about seven years and the three dormitories have a capacity of about three hundred beds. It is located on 440 acres of land. This has been the most miraculous work we have ever seen and has been fought and despised by the devil. I have never seen such miracles in all of my ministry.

The REBEKAH CHRISTIAN ACADEMY is the school for the Rebekah Home. It has a beautiful two story, air-conditioned building with the finest of equipment.

From 1961 to 1973 Roloff was developing these varied enterprises and ministering as an evangelist in many churches, plus carrying on his radio ministry. He was an experienced pilot, having flown about 12,000 hours in his 1966 Queen Air that a friend helped him to get, and also his 1968 Cessna Skywagon that was used for Lighthouse work which could land on the beach with people and provisions. These plans belonged to the Enterprise and had their own mechanic and radio men to maintain them and help fly them. Roloff landed his plane at least four times on one engine, and in unusual places such as a highway. His flying lessons began in 1958.

His themes all through the years were *"Christ is the Answer* and *"Now the Just Shall Live by Faith."*

The last of his varied works of good will--which, by the way, make no charges for those that they help, is the Rebekah Home in Corpus Christi which has been the scene of recent controversy. This was founded in 1967 along with the Peoples Church, a place where girls in trouble can worship as they get straightened out. This school specializes in taking cases other agencies and homes refuse to take. And no wonder--Roloff got results. He ran his schools by Bible directives and naturally got Bible results--changed lives. Over $3 million dollars was tied up in the Rebekah project alone.

In September 1970 the Gulf Coast storm *"Celia"* hit but miraculously did not touch the Lighthouse nor their home, although severe damage was most everywhere else. In 1971 their homes were filled to capacity, and they had to start turning people away. In May 1972, the Roloffs moved into their lovely large new home on the acreage where the Rebekah Home and other buildings were already located. Another 118 acres of land was purchased. it had a runway on it for their plane, and they could farm some of the remaining acres. During the summer of 1972, workers built another big two-story building, which became the Rebekah Christian School.

At the close of 1972, they had four days of dedication for the following new items: Chapel at the Intracoastal Canal; their new; the land adjoining the Enterprises property; a big new boys' home at Zapata, Texas; five new units at the Peaceful Valley Home; the high two-story dormitory at the Rebekah Home; the two-story Rebekah School; and the People's Church, which is nearly two blocks long.

The battle with the State of Texas developed ironically out of one of the most compassionate ministries done anywhere. Rebekah Home was founded as a place to help girls in trouble by giving them the answer which is Christ. A Dallas probation officer attests to the fact the place to send young people in trouble is Roloff's work. Children rejected elsewhere are welcomed with open arms and a book could be told of the amazing changed lives. Some of the young men from the Lighthouse have married some of the girls from Rebekah Home (the bumble bees meet the honey bees).

The talk of licensing began in 1971 which threatened to shut the work down unless they conformed to rules and regulations that would have greatly increased the cost of the operation without improving on what they were doing. Roloff's legal problems began in April 1973 when the state welfare department filed a suit in an attempt to have his Rebekah Home licensed. Had Roloff agreed to do this, he would then have had to follow welfare department guidelines, which would be totally alien to Bible principles and philosophy upon which the girls' home was founded. Roloff had no desire to fight the welfare department or put them out of business, but simply wanted this unconstitutional interference to stop. It is government interference with religion. "Licensing a church home is as unnecessary and wrong as licensing a church" Roloff contended. At issue is the constitutional principal of separation of church and state.

If licensed, the home would be required to hire a home supervisor who holds a degree in social work and who is approved by the welfare department.

That supervisor would be required to complete an additional fifteen hours of college level social studies every two years. Not only that, but the home would be required to file financial reports regularly with the state welfare department. The home would also have to hire one state-approved worker for every eight girls. The home would also be forced to serve foods from a menu prepared by the welfare department. The welfare department also objects to Bible discipline, which would have to be eliminated. One could readily see that Roloff would not be running the home he gave birth to, so naturally he chose to fight this invasion of privacy. When the welfare officials appeared, he asked them what they wanted. When they presented new rules, he simply took out his Bible and told them he was satisfied with God's rules.

On August 3, an injunction was signed in which Roloff was enjoined from operating a child care institution without a license for those under sixteen years of age. On October 5, 1973, a district judge heard the case and fined Roloff $500 and $80 court costs for contempt of court when he refused welfare guidelines. With Roloff refusing to have the home licensed, the welfare department leveled charges of brutality against the home based upon the testimony of a few of the girls. This adverse publicity was widespread. It was found that of the 1,500 girls who have spent time at Rebekah Home, fewer than a dozen could be found that would testify against it. One set of parents was found willing to testify for the welfare department. None of the 1,490 who were helped or thankful for the home or their parents were consulted.

Finally on January 31, 1974, the case went to court again in Corpus Christi and Roloff was found guilty--fined $5,400 and sentenced to five days in the county jail on contempt of court charges. The court also ordered him to "purge the home" which would mean to "dump the girls into the street." On February 4, he was given the opportunity to present his argument on the constitutionality of state licensing of a church- operated home before the Provisions Committee of the Texas Senate. What was to have been a five-minute presentation blossomed into a three-hour session when the senators began questioning Roloff on the accomplishments and problems of Rebekah Home. His jail term was limited to one day, February 12, pending appeal to the Texas State Supreme Court, and the fine was stayed as well, pending appeal. He was released from jail on a writ of habeas corpus.

On March 24, 1974, Roloff and his attorneys appeared before the nine judges of the State Supreme Court of Texas in a hearing to determine if a discharge of the charges could be obtained. This request was made on the grounds that the judgment was ambiguous and unclear in that it does not define what age constitutes a child or children. The former policy was that individuals up to age sixteen were considered children, but a recent state attorney general's ruling stated a person to be a child up to age eighteen. Questions were also raised in the minds of the judges as to what constituted a child care home. Answers were unclear from the welfare department and in one instance, contradictory. The high court agreed that children sixteen or over could be cared for by Roloff and, as a result, overturned the contempt of court charges May 20, 1974. Roloff received the news May 29 while at Bob

Jones University in Greenville, South Carolina, receiving an award "for those who have made special contributions to the defense of the faith." The Austin decision of the Supreme Court, however, did not end the fight.

The welfare department had been adamant in getting the under eighteen years of age law declared as needing a welfare license. Roloff continued to help girls of any age that came to him for help. He estimated that while he couldn't actively recruit for the younger ages, had there been no harassment, he could have handled up to 700 young people over against his approximate 200 that were now cared for.

To illustrate the problem, two girls, ages 13 and 15, ran away after two warnings for other offenses. They were told they would be spanked for the next violation. They were found four days later in a locked bar. They had spent this time with ten men and had a woeful story to tell. Roloff kept his word and spanked them. Word got out about the incident and Roloff was served a summons for child abuse. At the hearing the girls admitted the offenses and the spankings. The judge declared Roloff could keep them until the trial. Roloff refused until the judge would ask them a question as to where they would like to go--back to Roloff or to some alternate arrangement. Hugging their "daddy" with great affection, they said they wanted to be with Brother Roloff.

By March 1975, the Texas Welfare Department had filed against Roloff again for contempt and for being in violation of their rules and regulations. They had built up to 200 girls at Rebekah Home, half of what they had previously when forced to close. Even more tragic is that they turned away 3,000 during this time.

A legislative bill slipped through the Texas Senate on March 13, 1975, clearly aimed, many people feel, at outlawing his homes and work. It passed through the Texas House in May 1975. In June another court order was issued whereby Roloff would be held in further contempt if he did not allow inspection of the premises of their homes. He allowed the inspections having nothing to hide.

On July 4 and 5, 1975, a great rally was held in Garland and Dallas where hundreds of people gathered to join in the battle with such as Jack Hyles and Bob Jones III addressing the crowds. On July 25, shortly thereafter, the Lighthouse dormitory burned to the ground. Later a tall boy got saved and confessed to setting the fire.

It seems that Roloff's case was being considered a test case by many. What happens may determine the ultimate status of many other preachers.

By January 1, 1976, the new guidelines by the welfare department become law, making it illegal for unlicensed homes to take in children under the age of eighteen. In May 1976 a judge's order instructed Roloff Enterprises to allow state welfare workers to inspect the homes. This time Roloff refused. On June 3 a great rally with some 400 people was held in Austin, preceding Roloff's court appearance to fight state licensing. Again he was put in jail on June 21. He was released June 25, just prior to his 62nd birthday. He was fined $1750. In the fall of 1976 a final ruling was laid down giving him freedom until the

Supreme Court of the United States would hear his case.

On November 1, 1977, a great freedom rally was held at the convention center in Dallas. Great crowds came including over 1,500 preachers and public sentiment again swelled for Roloff. Nearly a year later, on October 2, 1978, the Supreme Court ruled against hearing the case from Corpus Christi. Attorney General John Hill of Texas said the case was frivolous, and the justices must have believed it. Appearing on nationwide television "60 Minutes" with Mike Wallace on October 22 gave Roloff some national favorable coverage long overdue. Then on November 7 this same thorn-in-the-flesh Hill was defeated in his bid for governor of Texas by William Clements in a very close election. Elements had indicated he would use his powers to free Roloff from all charges. Perhaps justice would still be mete out.

Roloff's battle with Texas authorities continued through most of his life. There were times when things were calm, and times when he was in court or in jail.

On the way to a meeting he with three of his staff flew into some turbulent weather and it is conjectured a wing disengaged from his aircraft. This was the end as the plane plummeted to earth killing all of the occupants. On the day of his death it was an ironic turn of events, for his chief antagonist, Mark White, was elected governor of Texas. Long time friend, Jack Hyles conducted the funeral a couple days later in a civic auditorium in Corpus Christi, Texas. The work with some modifications has carried on, but some facilities have been terminated and moved to other states.

The Life
And Ministry Of

Rodney (Gipsy) Smith
1860 ~ 1947

RODNEY (GIPSY) SMITH

BORN: March 31, 1860
Wanstead, England

DIED: August 4, 1947
Atlantic Ocean

LIFE SPAN: 87 years, 4 months, 4 days

Gipsy Smith was perhaps the best loved evangelist of all time. When he would give his life story, the crowds that came to hear usually overflowed the halls and auditoriums. His trips across the Atlantic Ocean were so numerous that historians seemingly disagree on the exact number.

Born in a gypsy tent six miles northeast of London at Epping Forest, he received no education. The family made a living selling baskets, tinware and clothespegs. His father Cornelius and his mother Mary (Polly) Welch provided a home that was happy in the gypsy wagon, despite the fact that father played his violin in pubs at this time. Young Rodney would dance and collect money for the entertainment. Yet he never drank or smoked, which may have contributed to his longevity.

Cornelius was in and out of jail for various offenses, usually because he couldn't afford to pay his fines. Here he first heard the gospel from the lips of a prison chaplain. He tried to explain to his dying wife what he heard.

Rodney was still a small lad when his mother died from smallpox. A child's song that she had heard sung twenty years previous about Jesus came back to her, comforting her as she passed on. Her dying words were, "I believe. Be a good father to my children. I know God will take care of my children." Rodney never forgot seeing his mother buried by lantern-light at the end of a lane in Hertfordshire. God did take care of the children as the four girls and two boys (Rodney was the fourth child) grew up under the stern eye of their father. They all went into Christian service.

Following his wife's death, Cornelius had no power to be good. One day he met his brothers, Woodlock and Bartholomew, and found they too hungered after God. At a tavern at the Barnwell end of town they stopped and talked to the woman innkeeper about God. She groaned that she was troubled also and ran upstairs to find a copy of *Pilgrim's Progress.* Hearing this read to them, they decided this was what they wanted. Cornelius encountered a road worker who was a Christian and inquired where a gospel meeting might be found. He was invited to the Latimer Road Mission where he eagerly attended the meeting with all his children. As the people sang the words, "I do believe, I will believe that Jesus died for me," and *There is a Fountain Filled With Blood,* Cornelius fell to the floor unconscious. Soon he jumped up and said, "I am converted! Children, God has made a new man of me. You have a new father!" Rodney ran out of the church thinking his father had gone crazy. The two brothers of the father were also converted, (Bartholomew the same night). Soon the three formed an evangelistic team and went roaming over the countryside preaching and singing the gospel. Now Cornelius would walk a mile on Saturday night for a bucket of water rather than travel on Sunday! From 1873 on, "The Converted Gypsies" were used in a wonderful way with

Cornelius living until age ninety-one.

Soon after their conversion, Christmas came and the six children asked their father, "What are we going to have tomorrow?" The father sadly replied, "I do not know, my boy," The cupboard was bare and the purse was empty. The father would no longer play the fiddle in his accustomed saloons. Falling on his knees, he prayed, then told his children, "I do not know what we will have for Christmas dinner, but we shall sing." And sing they did. . . .

Then we'll trust in the Lord,
And He will provide;
Yes, we'll trust in the Lord,
And He will provide.

A knock sounded on the side of the van. "It is I," said Mr. Sykes, the town missionary. "I have come to tell you that the Lord will provide. God is good, is He not?" Then he told them that three legs of mutton and other groceries awaited them and their relatives in the town. It took a wheelbarrow to bring home the load of groceries and the grateful gypsies never knew whom God used to answer their prayers. Prayer now took on a new meaning as the teenager heard father pray, 'Lord, save my Rodney."

Rodney's conversion as a sixteen year old came as a result of a combination of things. The witness of his father, the hearing of Ira Sankey sing, the visit to the home of John Bunyan in Bedford all contributed. Standing at the foot of the statue of Bunyan, Smith vowed he would live for God and meet his mother in heaven. A few days later in Cambridge, he attended the Primitive Methodist Chapel on Fitzroy Street. George Warner, the preacher, gave the invitation and Rodney went forward. Somebody whispered, "Oh, it's only a gypsy boy." This was November 17, 1876, and he rushed home to tell his father that he had been converted. He got a Bible, English dictionary and Bible dictionary and carried them everywhere causing people to laugh. "Never you mind," he would say, "One day I'll be able to read them," adding, "and I'm going to preach, too. God has called me to preach." He taught himself to read and write and began to practice preaching. One Sunday he went into a turnip field and preached to the turnips. He would sing hymns to the people he met and was known as the singing gypsy boy. At seventeen, he stood on a small corner some distance from the gypsy wagon and gave a brief testimony. . .his first attempt at preaching.

One day at a convention at the Christian Mission (later the Salvation Army) headquarters in London, William Booth noticed the gypsies and realized that young Rodney had a promising future. He asked the young lad to preach on the spot. Smith sang a solo and gave a good testimony. Though he didn't try to be funny, there was a touch of sunshine in his ministry. On June 25, 1877, he accepted the invitation of Booth to be an evangelist with and for the Mission. His youngest sister was converted in one of his early meetings. For six years (1877-1882) he served on street corners and mission halls in such areas as Whitby, Sheffield, Bolton, Chatham, Hull, Derby and Hanley.

He was married on December 17, 1879, to Annie E. Pennock, one of his converts from Whitby, and their first assignment together was at Chatham.

Here the crowd grew from 13 to 250 in nine months. Their first child, Albany, was born December 31, 1880. Then it was six months in Hull in 1881. Here the name "Gipsy" Smith first began to circulate. Meetings at the Ice House grew rapidly and soon 1,500 would attend an early Sunday prayer meeting. A meeting for converts drew 1,000. Then came Derby with defeats and discouragements. However, the Moody 1881 visit in London was a big encouragement. Their last move was to Hanley in December 1881. He considered this his second home for the rest of his life. By June 1882, great crowds were coming and the work was growing. On July 31 a gold watch was given him and about $20.00 was presented to his wife by the warm-hearted folks there. Acceptance of these gifts was a breach of rules and regulations of the Salvation Army, and for this, he was dismissed from them. The love in Hanley was returned by Smith, for when his second son was born on August 5, he named him Alfred Hanley. His eight assignments with the Salvation Army had produced 23,000 decisions and his crowds were anywhere up to 1,500.

Now Cambridge became Gipsy Smith's permanent home for the rest of his life. However, the urging of the people at Hanley to return as an independent preacher was strong. So he returned--ministering there for four years. Crowds reached 4,000 at the Imperial Circus building which was used for three months during this time. These were the largest crowds in the country outside of London. At one pre-service prayer meeting in 1882, the crowd of 300, including Smith, toppled to the room below as the floor collapsed under them injuring seventy people! In 1883 came his first trip abroad with a visit to Sweden and on February 1, 1884, his third child was born. . .a girl named Rhoda Zillah. His brief appearance on the program of the Congregational Union of England and Wales Convention swamped him with several offers. Because of this, he traveled extensively from 1886 to 1888, hampered for nine months during 1886 with a throat ailment.

On January 18, 1889, Gipsy Smith left Liverpool for his first trip to America arriving later in the month on a wet Sunday morning. He didn't know a soul in America. He had nothing but credentials from friends back home which he used to introduce himself to some church leaders. Similar to Moody's experience some years earlier in England, the ones who had originally invited him had either died or become indifferent. Dr. Prince of the Nostrand Avenue Methodist Episcopal Church of Brooklyn opened up his pulpit for a three week crusade with him. The 1,500 seat auditorium was jammed and between 300 to 400 people found the Lord. Following this, he traveled from Boston to San Francisco thrilling large audiences with his story and message. When he returned to England later in the year, he became assistant to F. S. Collier, of the Manchester Wesleyan Mission. Meetings were greatly used of God in a ten day campaign there. The midnight service saw people leaving theatres and bars to come in. Busy as he now was, he never grew tired of visiting gypsy encampments whenever he could on both sides of the Atlantic.

His second trip to America was in August 1891. The old James Street Methodist Church of New York, with Pastor Stephen Merrit, hosted his first meeting in September. There was a great revival. He went to Ocean Grove,

New Jersey, a Methodist camp ground with a 10,000 seat auditorium. After a couple sermons here where he made many new friends, he returned to the Brooklyn church mentioned previously for a repeat crusade. Then a month long crusade was held at the Calvary Methodist Episcopal Church of New York with Pastor James Roscoe Day. Many were saved. A good series followed back in Edinburg, Scotland, in 1892. From this series came the Gipsy Gospel Wagon Mission, devoted to evangelistic work amongst his own people.

In 1892, he took his third trip to America, this time with his wife. He was invited to hold special "drawing room meetings" for some of the elite in one of the largest mansions on Fifth Avenue in New York City. It was not a public meeting, but personal letters were sent to various aristocratic ladies of New York, inviting them to be present. There were to be six meetings and at the first there were 175 ladies present. Facing Mrs. John D. Rockefeller and such, he simply preached on "Repentance." He said, "I only remembered that they were sinners needing a Savior." He visited Ocean Grove, Lynn, Massachusetts, and Philadelphia in meetings sponsored by the Methodists. The newspaper coverage was good to Gipsy in a united campaign in Yonkers, New York. Denver, Colorado, was exceedingly generous to them. From September 1893 to January 1894, he returned to Glasgow, Scotland, for a seven week crusade in seven different churches over a five month period. The whole city was stirred.

On May 22, 1894, Gipsy Smith arrived in Australia and began a six week campaign in Adelaide. Then on to Melbourne and Sydney where he received a cable that he wife was very sick. This aborted his visit here after only three months, but 2,000 people came to his sendoff. Stopping in New York, the news was that his wife was some better, so he spent time at Ocean Grove and in an Indianapolis crusade. It was here that an old man felt Gipsy's head saying, "I am trying to find your bumps, so that I can find the secret of your success." Smith replied, "You must come down here," and placed the man's hand upon his heart. Home in November, he found his wife regaining her health. In 1895, he went to London for three months and then on to Alexander MacLaren's church in Manchester. Thorough preparation here produced 600 converts in an eight-day meeting. Then it was on to other towns, Swansee, Wales, and back to Edinburg, Scotland.

On January 1, 1896, he made his fifth trip to America and held a great campaign in the People's Temple in Boston. This was the city's largest Protestant Church, with Pastor James Body Brady. Gipsy saw a sign outside the church, *Gipsy Smith, the Greatest Evangelist in the World.* He made them take it down. The four week crusade went seven weeks with 800 being received into the church. He then had a good campaign with Pastor Hugh Johnstone at the Metropolitan Episcopal Church of Washington, D.C. There he met President Grover Cleveland, one of the two presidents he was to meet, and also had blind 70 year old Fanny Crosby on his platform one night singing one of her hymns. Upon his return home, he was made a special missionary of the National free Church Council from 1897 to 1912. Staying in England for awhile, his 1899 crusade at Luton had 1,100 converts and his 1900 crusade at the Metropolitan Tabernacle in London had 1,200 converts. A Birmingham, England, crusade resulted in 1,500 converts.

One of the highlights of his life was his trip to South Africa in 1904 (age 44). He took his wife along. His daughter Zillah was the soloist. They spent six months there. He closed out in Cape Town on May 10, seeing some 3,000 come to the inquiry rooms during his crusade there. A tent meeting in Johannesburg started on June 9 in a 3,000 seat tent. He finally left in September and it was estimated that 300,000 attended his meetings with 18,000 decisions for Christ during the whole African tour.

The 1906 crusade in Boston, Massachusetts, was one of his most renown. Under the auspices of the Boston Evangelical Alliance and personal sponsorship of A. Z. Conrad, Smith conducted 50 meetings at Tremont Temple attended by 116,500 people. Decision cards totaled 2,290.

In 1908 and 1909 France was his burden. Speaking to the cream of society at the Paris Opera House, he saw 150 decisions made. In 1911 and 1912 he was back in America working with the Men and Religion Forward Movement. During World War I, he was back in France beginning in 1914 and for three and one half years ministered under the Y.M.C.A. auspices to the English troops there, often visiting the front lines, resulting in receiving the Order of the British Empire which George VI made him a member of.

In 1922 the Nashville, Tennessee, crusade seemed to achieve great heights of pulpit power. He had 6,000 Negroes out at a special service.

Once when preaching to Negroes only in Dallas, someone called out, "What color are we going to be in heaven? Shall we be black or white?" Gipsy replied, "My dear sister, we are going to be just like Christ."

An "amen" rang out all over the hall.

In 1924 his crusade at the Royal Albert Hall in London had 10,000 attending nightly for the eight day meeting.

In 1926 he made his second trip around the world. In Australia and New Zealand, radio greatly enlarged his ministry. In seven months he accumulated 80,000 decision cards from the large cities such as Sydney, Melbourne, Auckland, etc., as well as in areas of Tasmania. His twenty-fifth trip to the U.S.A. was in 1928 with his son Albany, who was also a preacher. They visited many churches. In Long Beach, California, he preached in a tent seating over 5,000. He also visited Toronto for the first time since 1909.

England was not responding to union crusades which Smith deemed necessary, so he was back in America in 1929. Now almost seventy, he traveled from Atlanta to Los Angeles with great power. He spoke to 10,000 people in Ocean Grove. San Antonio, Texas, had 10,000 decision cards signed in three weeks. One of his greatest Crusades was held in Winston-Salem, North Carolina, in a tobacco warehouse seating 6,000. Fifteen thousand attended his last meeting with the total of decision cards for the whole crusade being 27,500.

A large youth crusade was conducted in London in 1931. The year 1934 found him at an open air meeting near the spot where his gypsy mother died. Some 3,500 heard him. A church was started there as a result, called the North

Methodist Mission. In June 1935, he had a rally at Epping Forest near the spot where he was born. Ten thousand showed up to hear him talk about his life. His 1936 tour of America featured a great crusade in Elizabeth, New Jersey, with 5,000 attending the last night which was the 60th anniversary of his conversion! Hundreds were saved. His favorite song, *He Is Mine,* was sung. Another great Texas crusade held at Dallas in the Dalentenary Fair Grounds resulted in 10,000 decisions. Gipsy Smith's wife Annie died in 1937 at the age of 79 while he was in America. All of their children turned out well: a minister, an evangelist and a soloist. Harold Murray was his constant friend and biographer for thirty years and was pianist for him starting with the first World War.

Front page headlines on June 2, 1938, carried the news of the 78 year old widower marrying Mary Alice Shaw on her 27th birthday. This, of course, brought some criticism. But it was a good marriage for she helped him in his meetings, sang, did secretarial work and later nursed him when his health failed. He toured the United States and Canada from 1939 to 1945. In 1945 they went back to England. He preached a bit, but the country was pre-occupied with recovery from the war.

Gipsy was now very tired; and thinking the sunshine of Florida might be good for his health, they embarked again for America. Three hours out of New York, he died on the Queen Mary, stricken by a heart attack. Some say this was his 45th crossing of the Atlantic. His funeral was held August 8, 1947, in the Fifth Avenue Presbyterian Church of New York. A memorial with a plaque was unveiled on July 2, 1949, at Mill Plain, Epping Forest, England, his birthplace. So ends the life of one who once said, "I didn't go through your colleges and seminaries. They wouldn't have me. . .but I have been to the feet of Jesus where the only true scholarship is learned." And learned it was, --to even compel Queen Victoria of England to write him a letter. Gipsy never wrote a sermon out for preaching purposes. Only once did he use notes when he needed some Prohibition facts.

Smith wrote several books: *As Jesus Passed By* (1905), *Gipsy Smith: His Work and Life* (1906), *Evangelistic Talks* (1922), *Real Religion* (1929), *The Beauty of Jesus* (1932) and *The Lost Christ.*

He could sing as well as he preached. Sometimes he would interrupt his sermon and burst into song. Thousands wept as he sang such songs as, *Guide Me O Thou Great Jehovah* with tears running down his cheeks, or such as *This Wonderful Saviour of Mine* and *Jesus Revealed in Me,* a song that he wrote.

Christ the Transforming Light, Touches this heart of mine,
Piercing the darkest night, Making His glory shine.
Chorus:
Oh, to reflect His grace, Causing the world to see,
Love that will glow Til others shall know
Jesus revealed in me.

Another song that he wrote was *Not Dreaming.* This was written while he was resting in a corner of a railway compartment. He was reflecting on all the wonderful events of a recent campaign and some teenagers said, "Oh, he's only dreaming." He soon had a song to give the world. . .

> *The world says I'm dreaming, but I know 'tis Jesus*
> *Who saves me from bondage and sin's guilty stain;*
> *He is my Lover, my Saviour, my Master,*
> *"Tis He who has freed me from guilt and its pain.*

Chorus:

> *Let me dream on if I am dreaming;*
> *Let me dream on, My sins are gone;*
> *Night turns to dawn, Love's light is beaming,*
> *So if I'm dreaming, Let me dream on.*

Other hymns written were, *Thank God for You,* and *Mother of Mine.* C. Austin Miles wrote *But This I Know,* and dedicated it to Smith.

Although he was a Methodist, ministers of all denominations loved him. It is said that he never had a meeting without conversions.

The Life
And Ministry Of

Oswald Jeffery Smith
1889 ~ 1986

OSWALD JEFFERY SMITH

BORN: November 8, 1889   **DIED:** January 25, 1986
Odessa, Ontario, Canada   **Toronto, Ontario, Canada**
LIFE SPAN: 96 years, 3 months, 17 days

Pastor, evangelist, missionary statesman, author, hymn -writer, world traveler, poet, editor -- Oswald J. Smith is one of the most versatile Christian leaders in the history of the Christian church. Perhaps never has one man done so many different things well. It all centered in Toronto, Ontario, where Smith pastored from 1915 to 1959. He raised some fourteen million dollars for foreign missions, more than any other pastor in history. Half of this was from his own church. Smith was born at home above the train station.

Smith was a country boy and the eldest of ten children, the sixth son of Benjamin and Alice Smith. The father was a telegraph operator for the Canadian Pacific Railway. The family moved from Odessa to Walkerville to Woodstock and finally to Embro. Delicate in health most of his life, he was not expected to live to manhood. He trudged one and a half miles to school and attended the local church and Sunday school. At age 13 his Sunday school teacher said, "Any of you boys might be a minister." He thought in that direction from that time on. His conversion at age 16 was the result of the Torrey-Alexander evangelistic team. He had been reading about the Torrey crusade in Toronto which the newspapers were describing. The reports of 3,000 gathering only 90 miles away challenged him to take a trip to Toronto. Attending the Massey Hall services for a few days, he was saved at the seventh service -- one for boys and young men only, held January 28, 1906. Torrey preached on Isaiah 53:5. He soon decided that Toronto was the place to get a job. For a while he identified with a group of Christians called the Hornerites. Soon he spoke to a couple of youth groups in Mount Albert where his family had now moved plus the Beverly Street Baptist Church in Toronto. He began to attend Toronto Bible College evening school. This helped fire him up so that he applied to the Presbyterian Church for a mission field appointment. They rejected the desires of the brash 18 year old. He then began to sell Bibles and was very successful in this venture. Then came another chance to preach - - at the Seven Methodist Church, plus two more services in near-by circuit churches the same day. He then got a call from the Bible Society in Vancouver and so he was off on a train journey of six days to western Canada. In September of 1908 he began his work at Prince Rupert Island working his way up the coast selling Bibles and making contacts for the local pastors, making calls in remote lumber camps and homes. He soon ended up at Port Essington some 30 miles away. For the next few months, Smith sold Bibles and preached to the Indians. He met a Methodist missionary, G. H. Raley, who wanted Smith as his associate to minister during the winter to the Indians at Hartley Bay. Smith got his supplies, which were $20 worth of food, a small cook stove, an axe, a hammer and nails, two quilts, a blanket, plus fifteen jars of fruit and jelly. Arriving at the village, he found it almost covered by deep snow and as bleak and barren as he had ever seen. Stoic Indians met him. That winter was the most difficult time of his life. Soaking clothes and nights of bitter cold followed as Smith fought with his stove in a desperate effort to keep the green wood burning and the small quarters warm. This experience drove him closer to the Lord and also gave him an empathy with missionaries and their problems for years to come. He started a Sunday school, preached twice on Sundays and four times during the week, plus teaching the Indian children at school. By April 1909 he resumed his work selling Bibles up and down the coast of British Columbia, plus preaching wherever he could.

Feeling the spiritual lack at the Manitoba school, he entered Toronto Bible College in the fall of 1910. By late November Smith was chosen, along with five other students, to be one of the speakers at the Students' Public Meeting. His subject was "A Call to the Foreign Field" for his interest in missions was now beginning to grow. On December 8, 1910, he surrendered completely to God. His diary states:

> The greatest struggle is over, I surrendered completely to
> God. I now trust that He will send me out to the foreign
> field. I do not care if my life is hidden away, unknown by
> the civilized world, as long as it is known to Him.

At age 21, in January of 1911 he decided to hold a revival in Toronto -- his first extended campaign. He used the Missionary Tabernacle, prepared 3,000 posters and prepared his messages. Five were saved and on Friday night Jennie Tyrell sang. Five years of courtship followed. Soon J. Wilbur Chapman and Charles Alexander held a large crusade in Massey Hall where Smith served as an usher and then as a counselor. Then in mid-summer 1911 he took a position with the Pocket Testament League of Canada to become their first traveling secretary which gave him exposure throughout various areas in Ontario. Then in November he became pastor of the Belwood (Ontario) Congregational Church. A second church at Garafraxa used his services simultaneously. Graduating from Toronto Bible College, he went off to Chicago in the fall of 1912 to begin studies at McCormick Theological Seminary, strong Presbyterian school in those days. In February of 1913 he assumed the pastorship of the Millard Avenue Presbyterian Church on Chicago's southwest side. He continued until May then decided he would minister amongst the hills of Kentucky. He was assigned to a place called Cawood, a very small hamlet consisting of a combined store -- post office and one house as home base. Again like British Columbia, it was a lonely ministry. Out of these experiences came some of his finest poems which set the tone for much of his writings in later years. Towards the end of the summer, revival transpired at a place called Turtle Creek. His next year at McCormick Seminary (1913-14) saw him pastor the South Chicago Presbyterian Church also. His engagement to Miss Tyrrell was broken by mutual agreement in March 1914.

He had begun to write verse in 1906 (age 17) and on September 5, 1914, he saw his first collection of hymns published. D. B. Tower had provided the music. Three days later he wrote a well known hymn, *Deeper and Deeper*. On

April 29, 1915, he graduated from McCormick Theological Seminary and on the following night he was ordained in the church where he pastored. That day he spent in prayer and he became convinced of two things -- his work would be world-wide in coverage and Toronto would be his home base. The congregation begged him to stay, but he felt impressed to take an associate pastor's position at the Dale Presbyterian Church in Toronto where J. D. Morrow pastored.

June 6, 1915, begins a life time of ministry in Toronto. Smith served with vigor at this work and was impressed with one -- Daisy Billings who was the senior deaconess at the church. By the spring of 1916 he was physically exhausted and had to take a complete rest and went to Clifton Springs, New York, for an extended vacation. On September 12, 1916, he married Daisy Billings in a ceremony at the church by their pastor, J. D. Morrow. Two thousand attended. Dale became the center of evangelism. Smith was learning fast from Morrow and soon was doing considerable preaching there. Morrow decided to become a chaplain in 1916 and Smith was made the pastor of this the second largest Presbyterian Church in Canada. In September of 1917 a real revival came to the church which prompted Smith to write, *A Revival Hymn*. Morrow returned only briefly but with failing health moved on to California to die in 1921. Smith's strong stand began to cause a concern amongst the liberal element as has happened so often in history. It was the irritating revival meetings, the use of gospel hymns, the prayer meetings, the $600 raised for missions. So in October of 1918 he terminated his ministry. Their first son, Glen was born June 22, 1917. A call was given to return to British Columbia under the Shantymen's Christian Association. Settling his family following their arrival on April 1, 1919, he began to preach to a needy and forgotten section of Canada's society. However, a vision of Toronto and its masses burned in his soul, so he returned later in the year and served in various Christian causes until it was God's time to open up the right doors. On February 4, 1920, his only daughter Hope was born. Smith spent part of this summer in Kentucky again.

Smith now 30 years of age decided it was time for action. Renting the West End YMCA, he started his own services in October of 1920 calling the work the Gospel Tabernacle. Sixty-four showed up in the 750 seat auditorium for the first service. Three months later this new work merged with the Parkdale C.M.&A. Church, and Smith became the pastor of the new work in January of 1921. On June 1, 1921, their third child Paul was born. He later would succeed his father as Pastor of the famed People's Church. A tent meeting to attract attention did just that when Smith had a "Bring your own chair" shower on Sunday, July 3. The tent was filled with every kind of kitchen chair imaginable. A new church was soon needed. For $40,000 they built an 80 foot by 130 foot auditorium seating 1,800. Paul Rader dedicated it on May 14, 1922, and the new work was called the Alliance Tabernacle. He packed the auditorium by giving the people something they could not get any other place -- variety. The best evangelists and singers in North America were constantly streaming across his platform. Establishing this kind of program made it easier for him to be gone weeks and months at a time later because the people were used to different men filling the pulpit. He was now getting calls for many ministries elsewhere. The Alliance Tabernacle of New York called him to succeed A.B. Simpson but he declined. One of the speakers at his church was William Fetler of the Russian Missionary Society who had a burden for the Russian origin populace of the Baltic countries who were ripe for the Gospel. Smith sailed on July 2, 1924, on his first of many trips outside the continent. Smith and Fetler had great meetings with many of the auditoriums seating over 2,000 in such places as Latvia and Poland. Back in Toronto with additional influence the church grew until at times 1,000 would be turned away from a service. Smith pioneered soul-winning in Toronto. Gospel singing, intense evangelistic crusades with a teaching ministry on Wednesday and Friday nights continued to inspire the Christians throughout the area. He resigned in 1926 and did a year's worth of evangelistic efforts. In April 1927 he accepted a call to The Gospel Tabernacle of Los Angeles, California. But Toronto was in his heart. Even though he was drawing crowds up to 2,200 and his church offered to build a 3,000 seat auditorium if he remained, he left in April 1928 to go "back home."

Most people start at the bottom and work up -- but not Smith. He rented Massey Hall and on September 9, 1928, at this first service he faced an audience of nearly 2,000 people. The Cosmopolitan Tabernacle was born. The crowds grew and so did the number of converts. On January 13, 1929, he was off to the Baltic countries for his second trip, now at the invitation of Paul Rader. He visited many countries this time. In Latvia over 2,000 were saved and one night a crowd of 1,300 sang his song *Saved*, which was the first time he had heard one of his songs in a foreign tongue. He returned to Massey Hall, then on March 30, 1930, they moved to a permanent address -- the empty 1,500 seat St. James Square Presbyterian Church on Gerrard Street East. It was now called the Toronto Gospel Tabernacle. He put the church on radio and kicked off the new work with a missionary convention. Soon it grew and he decided to move once again which he did to the empty Central Methodist Church on July 1, 1934. The name The People's Church, 100 Bloor Street East became famous from that time on. Smith was now pastoring the largest church in Canada and was often quoted in the media. Music was at its best, the Back Home Hour broadcast followed the evening service, the missionary conventions, the evangelistic crusades all helped bring in the crowds. The annual missionary conference, going often for a full month, was to eventually get $300,000 annually in Faith promise offerings, a technique Smith has widely and successfully utilized. The convention is loaded with mottoes and displays from various missionaries. A large thermometer tells the congregation how they were doing toward their goal.

Evangelism was emphasized. Soon nearly 500 were saved each year besides those in radio. Eldon B. Lehman was an early musical director and had a choir of 135 voices and an orchestra of 40 pieces. Sometimes the evening crowds would be higher than the morning. Curtailing newspaper advertising for several years did not hold the crowds back. They had a $40,000 pipe organ that took too much space so they sold it and built a second gallery. A 1944 evangelism crusade was moved to Massey Hall and eventually to Maple Leaf Gardens. Over 11,000 attended two Sunday nights.

On January 1, 1959, Smith turned over the reins to his son Paul while still enjoying such titles as founder, missionary pastor, pastor emeritus. It was in 1963 that the church was sold for $650,000 and a new church was built in the suburbs of Willowdale where he resides. The original investment in the former church was only $75,000 so that in essence Smith and his associates were given a brand new church worth $575,000 absolutely free. How can anyone else get something like this? Smith replies, "All you have to do is give 5 million dollars to foreign missions over a 25-year period and God will give a $500,000 church."

Smith's hymn writing has been an outlet for his feelings and emotions in hours of deepest depression and heartache. *Jesus Only* and *Christ is Coming Back Again* were some of the early songs. One of his songs, *Saved*, written in 1917 was the first of his hymns to gain universal attention. More than 1,200 hymn -poems followed with musical settings by Ackley, Stebbins, Harkness, Towner and other famed composers with C.M. Alexander as publisher.

After Towner and Alexander died, there was a lull until he met B.D. Ackley in 1930. Hymn after hymn Smith wrote and sent to him. Ackley provided music that fit the words and they began to be published by the Rodeheaver-Hall-Mack Company. From 1931 to 1946 there were 73 hymns that the two worked on together and that were successfully published. They became favorites over night and people everywhere were singing them.

Smith brought well known Christian songs to the public year after year. In 1931 *Joy in Serving Jesus*; 1931, *The Saviour Can Solve Every Problem*; 1933, *A Revival Hymn*; 1934, *The Glory of His Presence*; 1935, *Take Thou O Lord*; 1936, *His Love is All My Plea*; 1937, *God Understands*; 1938, *The Song of the Soul Set Free*; 1939, *The Need of the World is Jesus*; 1940, *Then Jesus Came*; 1941, *A Wedding Prayer*; 1942, *Surrender*.

His 1,200 hymns and poems made him one of the most widely used song writers. A few of the stories behind the hymns are *The Glory of His Presence* written in 1934 in the middle of the night. *God Understands* came as a result of Smith's youngest sister Ruth and her husband Cliff Bicker's plans to come home from Peru on their first furlough from missionary work. Just before leaving, Bicker was killed in an automobile accident. *Then Jesus Came* was written in 1939 in Philadelphia. Rodeheaver had asked for a song depicting the change in men when Jesus came. He soon had a new solo to sing. A.H. Ackley gave him the music for *The Song of the Soul Set Free* and soon had the words for this widely used choir number.

To sum it up seems as though you are describing the work of several men: As a pastor, Smith had ministered in Toronto since 1915. His congregation numbered about 3,500. About 2,000 attended the services, often three times a Sunday.

As an evangelist he has preached in the greatest churches in the world and held some of the largest campaigns ever held in many places of the world.

As a Missionary Statesman he has led his church in a program that now nets over $700,000 (growing each year) annually for foreign missions, more than any church on the face of the earth. The ratio in the budget being $7 to $1 in favor of foreign missions. This helps to support 350 missionaries from 35 faith missionary societies in 40 countries of the world. He has stimulated this kind of program via the Missionary Convention route in scores of churches.

As an author he has some 35 books out which have sold over a million copies. Produced by Marshall, Morgan and Scott of England the only author to surpass him in volume in the history of the publishing company is G. Campbell Morgan. His books, *The Passion for Souls* and *The Cry of the World* are the most challenging and practical books on missions ever written. Other titles are such as *The Man God Blesses, The Work God Blesses, The Revival We Need*, and scores more published in 128 languages.

As an editor he has published a magazine *(The People's Magazine)* for 36 years which enjoys a world wide circulation.

As a radio preacher his church services were carried by as many as 42 stations at a time. In later years he has conducted "Radio Missionary Conventions" in major cities across the United States and Canada challenging Christians and raising funds for the World Literature Crusade movement, of which he is honorary president.

As a world traveler he has toured 72 countries. His first major overseas tour was in 1924 when he visited nine countries in Europe.

Tours since then have included 1929 -- England, France, Belgium, Monaco, Italy, Austria, Germany, Latvia, Estonia, Lithuania, Spain, Poland and Switzerland; 1932 -- England, France, Spain, Egypt, Palestine, India, Ceylon, the Malay Peninsula, the Dutch East Indies, French Somaliland and Ethiopia; 1936 -- England, France, Spain, Germany, Poland, Latvia, Sweden, Denmark, Czechoslovakia, Romania, Bulgaria, Turkey, Greece, Yugoslavia, Hungary, Austria, Belgium and Scotland; 1938 -- Hawaii, Samoa, Fiji, Australia, the Solomon Islands and New Zealand; 1941 -- Jamaica; 1946 -- England, Ireland, Scotland and Wales; 1948 -- Ireland, England, Switzerland, Holland, Belgium, France, Italy, Germany, Iceland and back to Jamaica; 1949 -- Scotland, Ireland, England and Iceland; 1950 -- England, Belgium, Norway, Scotland, Germany and Denmark; 1955 -- Azores, Portugal, Senegal, Liberia, the Gold Coast, Congo, Northern Rhodesia, Southern Rhodesia, South Africa, Anglo-Egyptian Sudan, Egypt, Italy, France, England, Scotland and Newfoundland. Over 7,000 were converted in South Africa. 1957 -- Brazil, Argentina, Chile, Peru, Equador, Columbia, Panama. These were the largest united evangelistic campaigns in the history of South America which saw some 4,500 conversions. Here the 67 year-old Smith preached to crowds averaging 15,000 nightly at the Luna Park indoor fight arena in Buenos Aires, Argentina. Three times over 20,000 attended. Three hundred churches participated and over 1,500 decisions were registered here: 1959 -- Iceland, Norway, Sweden, Finland, England, Ireland and Scotland. During this trip he was received in Buckingham Palace. Then later in the year to Japan a campaign in Hong Kong preaching to 3,000 nightly and Hawaii; 1960 -- Alaska -- Japan where 1,000 decisions for Christ were made in the 2,200 seat Kyoritz Hall auditorium campaign in Tokyo. 1961 -- Hawaii, Fiji, Australia -- where over 1,000 young people volunteered for foreign service. Later in the year it was England, Germany, Italy, Kenya, Rhodesia, South Africa and Sudan; 1962 -- Iceland; 1962 -- Ireland, England and Wales. He nearly died on three of his trips because of poor health which has plagued him all his life. Why such energy and talent given so unreservedly to Christ? Smith replies with a motto he originated that has become world famous, "Why should anyone hear the Gospel twice before everyone has heard it once?"

On November 1, 1972, his beloved Daisy went to heaven after 56 years of marriage.

Smith preached his first sermon in a small Methodist Church in the village of Muskoka in 1908. Some 12,000 sermons later, he preached his last sermon at the Peoples Church in December 1981 at the age of 92.

Bedfast for the last months of his life, he died at the age of 96. His funeral was Thursday, January 20, 1986, at the Peoples Church in Toronto. It featured the singing of George Beverly Shea and the message of Billy Graham.

Now Oswald Smith experienced what he wrote:

"I have seen Him, I have known Him,
For He deigns to walk with me;
And the glory of His presence
Will be mine eternally.
O the glory of His presence,
O the beauty of His face
I am His and His forever
He has won me by His grace."

Dr. Oswald J. Smith's Favorite Missionary Mottoes

"You must go or send a substitute."

"If God wills the evangelization of the world, and you refuse to support missions, then you are opposed to the will of God.

"Attempt great things for God, expect great things from God."

"Why should anyone hear the Gospel twice before everyone has heard it once?"

"Give according to your income lest God make your income according to your giving."

"Now let me burn out for Christ."

"The Church which ceases to be evangelistic will soon cease to be evangelical."

"This generation can only reach this generation."

"The light that shines farthest shines brightest nearest home."

"Not how much of my money will I give to God, but, how much of God's money will I keep for myself."

"The supreme task of the Church is the evangelization of the world."

The Life
And Ministry Of

Charles Haddon Spurgeon
1834 ~ 1892

CHARLES HADDON SPURGEON

BORN: June 19, 1834
Kelvedon, England

DIED: January 31, 1892
Mentone, France

LIFE SPAN: 57 years, 7 months, 12 days

Considered by many to be the greatest preacher since the Apostle Paul, this English Baptist preacher was born of Huguenot origin the son and grandson of Congregational Independent ministers. His grandfather James Spurgeon pastored at Stambourne for 54 years (1804-58). His parents moved to Colchester where his father was in business and also preached at the Independent Church at Tollesbury. Charles lived with his grandfather in his earliest years (1835-41). He attended school at Colchester (1841-49) and in 1848 spent a few months at the All Saints Agricultural College at Maidstone. In 1849 he attended a Baptist school in Newmarket.

In spite of his background, Charles had not found the truth of the gospel for himself and as a teenager vowed he would visit every church in town to find out how to become a Christian. He heard one sermon on Galatians 6:7, but the preacher did not apply it personally and young Charles missed it again. After six months of visiting every chapel he could find, he was almost in despair. Evidently like Wesley, the preacher fathers were not versed in personal evangelism.

The cold, snowy morning of January 6, 1850, found him setting out to attend yet another church some distance away. As he trudged along his heart felt as cold as the falling snow. The fierce storm prevented him from reaching his destination and he turned aside into an obscure chapel he didn't know existed. It was the Artillery Street Primitive Methodist Church. He entered hesitantly as he had heard by reputation that Methodists sang so loudly that they made one's head ache.

A tall, thin man shuffled to the front and explained that the minister must have been held up by the weather so he would substitute. He quickly selected a text, Isaiah 45:22, *"Look unto Me, and be ye saved, all the ends of the earth."* Young Spurgeon noticed he could not even pronounce his words right. The substitute said repeatedly, "Look, it is just look!" Spurgeon wondered why he hadn't thought of that before. The preacher continued, "Look unto Me, I'm sweatin' great drops of blood! I'm hangin' on the cross!" He spotted Charles and said, "Young man, you look miserable...young man, look to Jesus Christ! Look! Look!"

Spurgeon was fifteen and testified later, "I saw at once the way of salvation. I looked until I could have almost looked my eyes away! The darkness rolled away and I saw the sun. I felt I could spring from my seat and shout with the wildest of these Methodist brethren, 'I am forgiven!'" The identity of the substitute preacher is still shrouded in mystery, but someone faithfully doing his duty the best he could is certainly shining as a bright star somewhere in God's Heaven.

"Oh, how I wish I could do something for Christ," he wrote to his mother.

Within a week, he had found something. First it was giving out tracts, then when his supply was exhausted he wrote on slips of paper and dropped them on the streets hoping someone could be helped.

The study of the scriptures led Charles to the conviction that he should be immersed and, later in 1850, he united with the Baptist communion from the Isleham Baptist Church. He was baptized by Pastor Cantlow on May 3, 1851. He joined the lay preachers association of the Baptist Church in Cambridge. He began teaching Sunday School and leading small prayer meetings there. His first sermon was preached in dignified surroundings in a cottage at Teversham near Cambridge, using I Peter 2:7 as his text. It was serious, practical and earnest. He would often walk ten miles to attend one of these short services.

Charles' gifts were quickly recognized and the fame of "the boy preacher" spread. In the evenings, after his school duties were over, he preached in chapels, cottages and out in the open air in as many as thirteen stations in the villages surrounding Cambridge.

In 1851 he was invited to deliver an address in a small Baptist church in Waterbeach not far away. There were less than a dozen in attendance. In 1852 that church called him to pastor. He was only 17 and probably the youngest minister in England. The church soon grew to 100. Despite his youth his pastoring showed signs of maturity and his extraordinary preaching ability was apparent. During this time, he lived in a different house nearly every day as some 52 families took him in. He served their about two years.

In 1853, Spurgeon gave a short address at the Cambridge Union of Sunday schools which led to his recommendation for candidacy at the New Park Street Chapel of Southward (south London). The once large Baptist church of Dr. John Rippon was about to close. Barely 20 he began his work there in mid 1854 with only 100 people in a 1,200 seat auditorium. Throngs of people were attracted to join the small congregation and before the end of the year the auditorium was too small.

One day, he announced that the church was going to have to be enlarged. Over the doubts of many parishioners remodeling began and the funds came in. Services were held in Exeter Hall during the renovation and the swelling crowds indicated that enlarging the old facility wasn't enough. A new tabernacle had to be built. On his 21st birthday he received the first gift toward this project. The enlarged chapel was crowded out before the new tabernacle was constructed. So in October of 1856 they temporarily relocated at the Royal Surrey Gardens Music Hall. At the first service, October 19, trouble makers came and cried, "Fire! Fire!!" Seven people were killed in the rush to vacate the premises and 30 seriously injured. It was estimated that 12,000 were in attendance.

Also in 1856 on January 8, Charles married a young lady in the church, Susannah Thomson who became a very effective helpmeet for him. Charles Spurgeon was not acclaimed as the "boy wonder of England." At 22, he was the most popular preacher of his day. The growing congregation steadily built the great Metropolitan Tabernacle located on Newington Causeway. The cost was $155,000. The seating capacity was 5,500 in the main auditorium, 146 feet long, 81 feet wide and 62 feet high. Having two galleries the building itself was 174' x 85'.

Charles spoke to his largest crowd, some 23,654 persons assembled in the Crystal Palace to join in the observance of the day appointed "for a solemn fast, humiliation and prayer before Almighty God in order to obtain pardon of our sins and for imploring His blessing and assistance on our arms for the restoration of tranquillity in India." This was Wednesday, October 7, 1857. He went to bed that night completely exhausted and didn't wake up until Friday morning.

In April 1858 there was another near catastrophe at Music Hall. Just as the last of the crowd was leaving, a part of the gallery gave way and came crashing down on the main floor because of heavy snow on the roof. Providentially, the auditorium was now empty...had it happened an hour earlier, hundreds would have been killed instead of the few fractured limbs that did result.

After almost five years at the Music Hall, the Metropolitan Tabernacle was opened on March 25, 1861...Spurgeon was 26. Here he would minister with great power and popular appeal until his death in 1892. One of his most memorable sermons, *"Baptismal Regeneration,"* was preached on June 5, 1864. An American visitor was once asked what he thought of Spurgeon after hearing him. "To tell you the truth, I was thinking of his Christ and not Spurgeon," he replied. It was Spurgeon who "painted pictures" while he spoke, ever pointing listeners to the Lamb of God with his knowledge of the Bible, his appropriate illustrations and timely admonitions.

In 1864, he revisited the chapel where he was saved and preached on Isaiah 45:22, again pointing to a seat under the gallery he said, "I was sitting right there in that pew!" That's where it all began.

He began to edit the monthly S*word and Trowel*, a church newspaper. His sermons soon found themselves also published by American newspapers. A lyceum official in America offered Spurgeon a contract for 50 nights at $1,000 per night to come to America and lecture. Spurgeon replied, "I can do better than that...I can stay in London and save fifty souls." And he surely did see souls saved. One girl, asking for membership in his church, was asked for evidence of her change in heart. "I have none except that now I sweep under the mats and rugs in the house where I am employed," the girl replied.

His preaching aside, Spurgeon also excelled in public prayer. His over 5,000 membership was meaningful to him, for it is said that he knew them all by name. One old lady whom he visited once made an impression upon him when she said, "Ah, Mr. Spurgeon, if Jesus Christ does save me He shall never hear the last of it!" He observed the Lord's Supper almost every Sunday either at home or in the tabernacle and he was a convinced Calvinist.

Besides the regular pastoral and preaching duties and publishing of weekly sermons (from 1855 on), he founded the Spurgeon's (pastor's) College in 1856. Nine hundred students were thus trained for the ministry under him. He told his students, "When you speak of heaven let your face light up and radiate with a heavenly gleam. Let your eyes shine with reflected glory...and when you speak of hell, well then your everyday face will do!" He also warned them, "Don't go out for popularity. Preach nothing down but the devil and nothing up but Christ." He also built a circle of Sunday schools and churches, was president of a society for the dissemination of Bibles and tracts and established Stockwell Orphanage with 12 houses in 1867 which accommodated 500 children.

Spurgeon refused to compromise just to stay a popular pulpit idol. Combining conviction and Bible-centered content in his sermons, he displayed a hard-core Calvinism which rejected both the sentimentalism and the rationalism infecting 19th century church thinking. He opposed the evangelical party of the Church of England on their doctrine of baptism and published his work on *Baptismal Regeneration* repudiating it. Withdrawing from the Evangelical Alliance because he distrusted the rising tendencies of modern Biblical criticism, he also deplored the Baptist's inclination toward the same and withdrew from the Baptist Union in 1887. He remained an ardent Evangelical and a staunch Baptist and Calvinist.

At this time the down-grade controversy, an assault on the basic doctrines of the faith commenced. Never desirous of making trouble for trouble's sake he once wisely said, "It is never worthwhile to make rents in a garment for the sake of mending them, nor to create doubts in order to show how cleverly we can quiet them." He lived in an era of great moral leadership in England with Queen Victoria and prime minister William Gladstone at the helm. Speaking of Gladstone he said, "We believe in no man's infallibility but it is restful to feel sure of one man's integrity."

Spurgeon always appealed to the scriptures as authoritative. His simplicity and voice were great assets to preaching. He excelled in his use of illustrations and anecdotes. A typical illustration would be, "A minister made up a generous purse of money to pay a widow's rent but when he knocked at her door there was no answer. Later when the widow was told who visited her she said, "I thought it was the man who came to collect the rent!" He was criticized in his day for his use of illustrations but like Jesus, he believed they had their place. He said using illustrations was like building a house with windows. Even in private he would illustrate scriptural truth. Once while speaking to a backslider about church attendance he was unable to get the response he wanted. Then without speaking he took a pair of tongs and lifted a live coal out of the fireplace. Both men watched as the flame and the coal became a dead black cinder. "You don't need to say anything more," the man protested, "I'll be back in my place next Sunday."

Wilbur Chapman, seeing the secret of his power, once quoted Spurgeon:
"Every day and night thousands of men and women here in
London pray for the work of the Tabernacle and for me. All
around the world, day after day, hundreds of thousands of
God's people ask for His blessing on me and my sermons. In
answer to those prayers, the Lord opens the windows of
heaven and pours out so many blessings that there is not

room in our hearts and lives to receive them all. Young man, try this way of running your church!"

Another time, when asked about the secret of his life, he said, "I looked at God and He looked at me and we were one forever."

During the last twelve years of their life together, Charles and his wife enjoyed a delightful residence at Nightingale Lane which he called "Westwood" located in Beulah Hill, a London suburb. They moved there in August 1880. His mother died in 1883.

Spurgeon invited the great evangelist Dwight L. Moody to preach in his tabernacle twice. The first time Moody flatly turned it down:

"In regard to my coming to your Tabernacle, I consider it a great honor to be invited, and, in fact, I would consider it an honor to black your boots; but to preach to your people would be out of the question. If they will not turn to God under your preaching, 'neither will they be persuaded, though one rose from the dead'."

Yours, with much love, D.L. Moody

The second time he accepted:

"I have for years thought more of you than of any other man preaching the Gospel on this earth, and, to tell you the truth, I shrink from standing in your place. I do not know of a church in all the land that I shrink from as I do from yours -- not but what your people are in sympathy with the Gospel that I try to preach, but you can do it so much better than I can.

I thank you for inviting me, and (D.V.). I will be with your good people November 20. Will you want Mr. Sankey or will your own precentor have charge? Either will suit me. Remember me to your good wife, and accept my thanks for your letter of cheer."

Yours truly, D.L. Moody

Spurgeon was grievously afflicted with a serious disease for several years and became an invalid for a number of months before his death at age 57. He had inherited the tendency for gout which, with a complication of other diseases, seemingly not clearly understood by his physicians carried him steadily downward. He was absent from his pulpit for most of the year preceding his death. Many a time he limped into his pulpit leaning heavily on his stick unable to stand, yet preached kneeling with one knee on a chair. But even then the astonished congregation saw him warming to his work, inspired by his all-consuming zeal push the chair aside and grasping the rail of the platform with both hands stand there for the rest of the service...apparently forgetful of his bodily distress.

His last sermon was preached June 7, 1891, to his 5,311 membership and friends at the Tabernacle:

"If you wear the livery of Christ, you will find Him so meek and lowly of heart that you will find rest unto your souls. He is the most magnanimous of captains. There never was His like among the choicest of princes. He is always to be found in the thickest part of the battle. When the wind blows cold, He always takes the bleak side of the hill. The heaviest end of the cross lies ever on His shoulders. If He bids us carry a burden, He carries it also. If there is anything that is gracious, generous, kind and tender, yea, lavish and superabundant in love, you always find it in Him. These forty years and more I have served Him, blessed be His name!...and I have had nothing but love from Him. His service is life, peace, joy. Oh, that you would enter in it at once! God help you to enlist under the banner of Jesus Christ!"

Spurgeon went to France for a vacation to try to regain his health, but at 11:05 p.m. on Sunday, January 31, 1892, he passed over to the other side. Memorial and funeral services at the Tabernacle from February 7 to 10 were probably attended by no less than 100,000 people. Charles' preaching Bible was placed on top of his casket, opened to Isaiah 45:22. Moody later received this Bible and consulted it often. His brother, James and his two sons, Charles and Thomas, were excellent preachers and carried on the work in Spurgeon's absence. Arthur T. Pierson was called to be his successor and served 1892-1903.

Spurgeon was never ordained by men. God called him to preach and the rest is history. Converts at the Tabernacle totaled 14,460 souls.

How was this Baptist preacher received by the state church of England? One of their clergymen said:

"There was an old preacher named Spurgey,

He had no use for liturgy

But his sermons were fine, I take them for mine,

And so does the rest of the clergy!"

Charles Spurgeon published more than 2,000 sermons, 63 volumes of sermons, commentaries, sayings, anecdotes, illustrations and devotions. His 49 volume set of *The Metropolitan Pulpit* was a mammoth work. His weekly sermons were published thus from 1855 on. Other writings included *The Treasury of David* (a homiletic commentary on the Psalms in seven volumes), *The Saint and His Saviour, Salt Cellars, Lectures to My Students, John Ploughman's Talks, Feathers for Arrows, Morning by Morning - Evening by Evening, John Ploughman's Pictures, The Clue of the Maze, My Sermon Notes, Storm Signals* and others. His writings have reached enormous circulation, seldom, if ever, matched by any other preacher.

The Life
And Ministry Of

Thomas Dewitt Talmage
1832 ~ 1902

THOMAS DEWITT TALMAGE

BORN: January 7, 1832   **DIED:** April 12, 1902
Gatesville (now Bound Brook), **New Jersey**   **Washington D. C.**
LIFE SPAN: 70 years, 3 months, 5 days

Talmage is considered by many as the greatest gospel preacher ever. His sermons are so loaded that it is hard to put them aside once you begin to read one. During his life time, he had more people reading his sermons than any man in history for some 3,000 newspapers published them in syndicated columns to audiences reaching up to 25,000,000 weekly. This went on for 29 years. The public simply demanded them. Upon meeting Spurgeon in 1872 Talmage said, "I read your sermons." Spurgeon replied, "Everybody reads yours." He pastored the Brooklyn Tabernacle for 25 years, built it three times and saw it destroyed by fire three times, the last time a few minutes after he preached his farewell sermon. It became the largest Protestant church in America.

Talmage was the last of a family of twelve children. The parents, David and Catherine (VanNeest) were godly Christians. The elder Talmage was an elder in the church through the years and serviced as a tollgate keeper, a farmer and the Sheriff of Somerset County, New Jersey. Four of his sons were to enter the ministry: James who died in 1879, Goyn who died in 1891 and John who died in 1892. Dewitt would be the youngest of the foursome and the most famous. His father read the Bible on his knees in the morning and his mother prayed and something good was bound to happen; others predicted a great future. Speaking of his youth he said, "I had many sound thrashings when I was a boy, but the most memorable scene in my childhood was that of father and mother at morning and evening prayers. I cannot forget it for I used to squirm around on the floor and look at them while they were praying."

He went through school in rapid style and at age 18 entered New York University to study law. However, the prayers of his parents that he should preach the Gospel soon prevailed for he was converted in the same year, 1850. Truman Osborne, an evangelist, came to his father's house and while the whole family was seated in the room said, "Mr. Talmage, are all of your children Christians?" Father said, "Yes, all but Dewitt." Osborne began to tell the story of the lamb outside the sheepfold that perished in the storm. He looked into the fireplace as he told the story, and Dewitt got the message and was saved. He stayed in a law office for three years. In 1853 he entered the New Brunswick Theological Seminary connected with Rutgers College. He later got a M.A. degree from NYU in 1862 although he did not graduate. Also the University of Tennessee gave him an honorary D.D. in 1884.

Dewitt wanted a chance to preach so he asked one of his theology professors if he would recommend him to a vacant pulpit of the Reformed Church at Belleville, New Jersey. He had been here and there as a preacher but this was his first sermon with considerable responsibility as he was now candidating for a church. He was soon to graduate from Seminary receiving his B.D. in 1856. He considered going to China where his brother was however, he prepared for his immediate challenge. He was ordained and installed as the pastor of the Belleville Reformed Church. His salary was $800 and a parsonage. This was on July 29, 1856. It was at Belleville that he married Mary Avery of Brooklyn by whom he had two children, Thomas and Jessie.

In 1859 Talmage accepted his second pastorate in Syracuse, New York, where a successful ministry followed at the Second Reformed Church. It was in Syracuse that he made his first public lecture - a literary lecture for which he was paid $50.

In 1861 when 29 years of age he received a call from the Second Reformed Church of Philadelphia. Six weeks of sleeplessness followed but he finally declined the call as a spirit of revival plus repairs on the building seemed to keep him in Syracuse. One year later in 1862 the call was again renewed and this time he moved to Philadelphia, installed on April 17th.

His young wife was tragically drowned in the Schuylkill River at Fairmount Park in Philadelphia shortly after his arrival. Somehow a terrible rumor was passed along that spread across the country that Talmage was sailing with his wife and her sister; that the boat capsized and having the opportunity of saving either his wife or her sister, he let his wife drown, saved the sister and married her in 60 days. Tens of thousands heard this report but the facts of course are contrary. The true account was that Talmage's sister, Sara Talmage Whitenack (and her daughter Mary) joined his wife and daughter for an outing at Fairmount Park. Talmage hired a boat for a ride and all got in. He knew nothing about the dam across the river until he saw someone wildly waving on the shore as though there was danger. Talmage looked back and saw he was in a current of the dam. With terror in his heart he tried to back the boat but in vain. The boat capsized and his wife instantly disappeared and her body was not found until days later. Talmage, unable to swim, had his niece hanging on, his sister Sara clinging to the other side of the boat and his own daughter more dead than alive also in the water. They were finally all rescued but this was a terrible disaster to go through. It all happened June 9, 1862.

Nine months after the tragedy in early 1863 a Susan C. Whittenmore of Greenpoint, New York, was introduced to him by his brother Goyn. She was a woman with considerable means and on May 7, 1863, the couple married where they met at the Greenpoint Dutch Reformed Church. She was to prove a most capable helpmate. This union had five children; May, Edith, Frank, Maud and Daisy. Susan was to live until 1895 and provide 32 happy married years.

While in Philadelphia he helped fortify the city against expected attacks from the Confederate army. During the war he also served as a chaplain in the Union army. The Civil War soon peaked and Philadelphia had many camps of prisoners, war hospitals for the sick and wounded and the like. Talmage was privileged to be of some service in the field for the Christian Commission and after the war he traveled in the South speaking on the need for reconciliation.

He now began lecturing on various causes although it was always subordinate to his chief work of preaching the Gospel. His lectures were once a week, usually on Thursdays. He has stated that lecturing saved his life and prolonged his work. The weekly railroad traveling was like a doctor's prescription that gave him just enough diversion to keep him fresh for his congregations. The prices paid him seemed too large to him but local committees desired to use him and did not object to his use of the lecture tours to say things that he could not say from the pulpit. His lecture platform gave him chances to meet with hundreds of thousands of people to whom, through the press, he presented the Gospel. For many years he had been paid from $400 to $1,000 for a single lecture averaging $500 per night. He was offered $6,000 for six lectures during the Chicago World Fair later in 1893 but he declined.

It was during the Civil War, when news was exciting, that a journalist would come to his church for a copy of his sermons. He spent the years 1862 to 1869 in Philadelphia. His church was a large one.

In February 1869, (37 years old) he received four calls simultaneously to four of the largest pulpits in America - Calvary Church of Chicago, the Union Church of Boston, the First Presbyterian Church of San Francisco and the Central Presbyterian Church of Brooklyn. One morning a committee from Chicago was in one room, a committee from Brooklyn in another room of his house and a committee from his own Philadelphia Church in another room. His wife passed from room to room entertaining them to keep the three committees from meeting.

On the train to Harrisburg for an engagement a voice spoke to him almost audible, "Go to Brooklyn." He was unanimously called on February 16, 1869, with a salary of $7,000 offered. On March 22 he was installed. The church was much smaller than the one in Philadelphia but there was a glorious opportunity for work in it. The church met in a large building but had only a small membership. Nineteen of 35 total membership signed the call. Within three months it was too small to hold the people who came there to worship. Soon a certain group of preachers began to slander him and lie about him, perhaps jealous of his success. These charges began to be published. The result was that the New York correspondents of the leading papers in the chief cities of the country came to his church on Sunday expecting Talmage would make counter attacks, which would be good news. Talmage never said a word in reply. Failing to get the sensational charges, they took down his sermons and sent them to the newspaper. So the falsehoods and persecution turned out for his advantage and enlarged his work. Soon his sermons would be regularly read by as many as 25,000,000 people per week in countries around the world as a result of the enemies' attempt to shut him up. Talmage was not quite happy about his church. He felt that people would come in and find things cold and stiff and go away never to come back. The church architecture was not conducive to a great home circle. He felt the church had to have a pulpit as a fireplace where everybody could gather around it and be warmed. An interdenominational Tabernacle began to be his burden. Within a year after coming to Brooklyn he projected, designed and established the Brooklyn

Tabernacle seating 3,500 people. The old Presbyterian Church was still utilized for other phases of the work. Prior to its dedication he left June 18, 1870, for a three month tour of Europe. Many subsequent trips followed. Back in the states on September 25, 1870, the first Brooklyn Tabernacle was dedicated. An offering of $13,000 was taken to help with the cost of the church. In less than a year the congregation had grown so large that the Tabernacle was enlarged and on September 10, 1871, it was re-dedicated with additional space now available. The offering this day was $21,000. The tabernacle in Brooklyn prospered because it was a soul-winning church.

The first of several fires burned the church down on December 22, 1872, after about one year of use. It happened early Sunday morning and it was providential none were yet in the church. Plans for a newer, larger, more complete Tabernacle were now formed.

Services continued at the Academy of Music Building in Brooklyn whose population of 300,000 constantly challenged him. The second Tabernacle was built seating 5,000. On January 22, 1874, it was dedicated and on February 22 it was open for worship. D. L. Moody's first large city-wide revival in November 1875 was a big encouragement during these days. But all was not quiet. A series of charges were made to the Brooklyn Presbytery in 1879 by some preachers saying such as Talmage's enthusiasm being sinful, his utterances inaccurate, his editorial work offensive but they were dismissed by a narrow margin as the people stood behind their pastor. The charges of "falsehood and deceit...using improper methods of preaching which tend to bring religion into contempt" have often been used against successful preachers.

In the spring of 1879 Talmage made a Gospel tour of England, Ireland and Scotland. From the time he began in London, June 15th, until he finished in Edinburgh he preached 98 times in 93 days. He confronted large audiences with nothing but the Gospel. A collection was always taken up for the benefit of local charities, feeble churches, orphanages, etc., Talmage donating his services. However, he also made 70 lectures and received $17,500.

Back home Talmage continued to lecture, preach and write. In 1883 the Brooklyn Bridge was opened and now Talmage's church was within fifteen minutes of downtown New York. By 1888 his salary was $12,000 with some $20,000 a year coming from lectures and $5,000 for editorship of a monthly journal. But the demand on him made him need all that he could earn. He received a tremendous amount of mail that needed to be answered and many other details that some would not think of, so when he was charged as being a millionaire clergyman it brought him great humor. Articles would begin, "The American preacher lives in a luxurious home" or "His income, from all sources, exceeds that of the President of the United States."

Talmage regretted that a minister of the Gospel could not accumulate money for himself, that he should not do so if he could. He worked hard, always had unfinished labors. He rose every morning at 6 a.m. He would take a morning stroll and go into a day's work. However on October 13, 1889, came a tremendous shock. The Tabernacle had burned to the ground the second time. Again it was an early Sunday morning fire but this time the causes were known. A thunderstorm from heaven and accompanying lightning and winds just tore up the facilities. He was scheduled to sail for the Holy Land on October 30 and only the encouragement of his trustees prevented him from canceling. In Palestine he baptized a man in the Jordan River causing further charges of being a sensationalist. Highlighting his return was his London meeting with Gladstone on January 24th. He returned in February 1890 and at the February 7th service held for his return at the Thirteenth Regiment Armory 7,000 gathered with big letters on the east wall saying, "Welcome." What a reception to a very worthy pastor! Services were held at the Academy of Music while the new Tabernacle was built. In the spring of 1891 (Easter Sunday) the third Brooklyn Tabernacle was opened. It was the biggest Protestant Church in the world. Talmage was now 59 years old. Thousands came to the three dedication services. $22,000 came in the offerings. It seated 6,000 but could hold 7,000. The cost was $400,000.

On June 15, 1892, he left for Europe again; this was his sixth trip. He began preaching June 25 in the City Temple of London his host being Joseph Parker. He also toured Ireland and Russia in the month of July. During a severe famine in Russia he had sent a shipload of flour to ease the famine. When in Russia he was received enthusiastically. Back to England where some crowds were estimated at 15,000 to 20,000 gathered to hear him. Back in Brooklyn he gave two years of his salary to the church to help pay for this huge debt that was incurred while building.

Talmage's voice came through loud and clear through the years against the corrupt politicians, the theater and infidelity that was causing people to forget God. He also founded and served as president of the Free Lay College while in Brooklyn.

On January 22, 1894, he made an electrifying announcement-resignation as pastor effective in the spring. He just felt 25 years in one place was sufficient. May 10-11 were made as sort of an international farewell and reception at the Tabernacle. The list of national and Christian dignitaries that took part was like a "Who's Who" gathering. Talmage's 25 years of work was finished. Who would now be able to succeed him, to even come close to filling the 6,000 seat auditorium?

The Lord must have known nobody for on May 13, 1894, one hour following the Sunday morning service and two days after his farewell, the Tabernacle burned to the ground for the third time. A fire started in the organ loft and soon it was all over. That morning Talmage had given his farewell sermon before departing on a journey around the world. Talmage narrowly escaped falling debris by the rear door of his church study. Over 6,000 had just left the premises. The adjoining hotel, Hotel Regent was also destroyed. Again no loss of life. On May 14th he began a previously scheduled round-the-world trip, arriving home in the fall. On January 6, 1895, he began a series of afternoon Gospel meetings in the Academy of Music in New York every Sunday. This was a temporary ministry until things crystallized. His weekly sermons for his world parish was a sacred obligation that he could not forego.

He had offers from nine churches in America and several in England for new pastorates but needed some time to reflect and continue his extensive literary work.

He had edited *Christian at Work* (1873-76), *Advance* (1877-78), Frank Leslie's *Sunday Magazine* (1879-89) and was now the editor of the *Christian Herald* since 1890. He authored a complete set of more than 500 sermons.

Besides the adjustment in leaving Brooklyn and finding God's next ministry, he experienced another upheaval in the passing of his beloved wife on August 5, 1895, who left him $200,000.

In October 1896 Talmage accepted a call to the First Presbyterian Church of Washington, D.C., to be co-pastor along with the aged Byron W. Sunderland, the President's pastor. He delivered a farewell address in Brooklyn at the Lafayette Avenue Presbyterian Church to 5,000 and then preached his first message in Washington on October 27th having been installed October 23rd.

Talmage was soon preaching Sunday mornings and evenings. He met his third wife -to-be in the summer of 1896 while she was visiting friends at East Hampton, Long Island, where Talmage often retreated to write and rest. She was Mrs. Charles Collier of Pittsburgh, a widow, and 39 years old when she married Talmage on January 26, 1898, in Pittsburgh. Talmage was 66 and beginning to tire and she became again just the mate he needed. Going west for a lecture tour in March was a real delight for the new bride. With so many demands on his time everywhere, he resigned the pastorate in March of 1899. In November, Talmage installed Donald McLeod as his successor in Washington. In April 1900 the Talmage's were off to Europe, another first for the new wife.

On July 8th he preached in the largest church in Sweden, the Immanuel Church of Stockholm, through an interpreter. His farewell service on September 30 at City Road Chapel in London (Wesley's chapel) had to have police control the crowds. They left October 18th for home. At the 20th anniversary of the Bowery Mission 10,000 heard Talmage at the Academy of Music in New York. In November 1900 another great crowd heard him at the Central Presbyterian Church in Brooklyn, his second visit back since the church burned. By now his mail was thought to be the largest received by any man in the country except for a few public officials; his sermons were now in 3,600 newspapers read by some 30,000,000 weekly. He knew every President of the United States well since James Buchanan. In March of 1901 he held a series of revival meetings in the Academy of Music in New York and thousands were saved.

The last sermon that he wrote was in February 1902 with the text being Psalms 33:2. His first trip to Mexico was basically for health and recreation. He did some preaching in Mexico City but was suddenly taken quite ill on March 3rd suffering an attack of influenza. Engagements had to be canceled as the party began the trip home. Talmage seemed well until reaching San Antonio, Texas, and fears then began to arise for his safety. He was under the constant care of a physician all the way home. A pain at the base of his brain gave evidence that a cerebral inflammation was taking place. Arriving home his condition worsened. His last words were to his daughter, "Of course I know you, Maude." Her wedding had just transpired. Two days before he died he lapsed into unconsciousness and around 9 p.m. passed on to the other side. The New York Times said, "The whole human race was his congregation." Funeral services were held at the Church of the Covenant in Washington on April 15th. He was buried in Greenwood Cemetery in Brooklyn.

The Life
And Ministry Of

Reuben Archer Torrey
1856 ~ 1928

REUBEN ARCHER TORREY

BORN: January 28, 1856   **DIED:** October 26, 1928
Hoboken, New Jersey   Asheville, North Carolina
LIFE SPAN: 72 years, 8 months, 28 days

Excellence in two areas of ministry has been achieved by a few; it has been a rare genius who has been so gifted in three areas but to excel in four capacities would seem near impossible...but it has been done two or three times in history. Reuben Archer Torrey is a classic example, for he was renown as an educator, a pastor, a world evangelist and an author.

Besides his obvious gifts in all these areas, he was also a man of prayer, a student of the Bible and an outstanding personal soul winner. It is said that he daily read the Bible in four languages, having a good working knowledge of Greek and Hebrew. Some students of church history feel he did more to promote personal evangelism than any other one man since the days of the apostles. His prayer life has seldom been equaled in the annals of Christendom.

One wonders if there has ever lived a man who did so many things well for Christ. One of his favorite phrases was, "I love to preach the Gospel of Jesus Christ."

Torrey was the son of a New York City corporation lawyer and banker. His parents, Reuben and Elizabeth, were refined and cultured Christians with mother spending much time in prayer for her son. The family moved to Brooklyn when he was three and when he was ten they moved again to a country home on 200 acres amid the uplands of the New York State. The fortune of the father was lost so that Torrey's eventual inheritance was only a matchbox and a pair of sleeve buttons. The Lord's Day was respected but somewhat lax restrictions the rest of the week produced a worldly teenager. Once in the attic he read a book that explained about being a Christian, but he felt God might make him a preacher rather than a lawyer so he determined not to follow through.

At age fifteen he was at Yale University and passed through a period of scholastic skepticism. His quick mind learned easily. He was an expert dancer and his conscience was not over sensitive about campus good times. "What more could I want?" he thought, "I've got all I need to make me happy." Social and worldly delights like race tracks, cards, the theater all crowded out any pursuit of Christian objectives.

One night at Yale he dreamed his mother came to him as an angel asking him to preach. His melancholy increased. He had a sudden impulse to commit suicide. He hurried to the washstand and fumbled for his razor or any other sharp instrument that would serve this purpose, but could not find a suitable weapon. His mother, miles away, was pulled from her bed by an invisible power to pray for her son whose faith had been shaken. Torrey, about to commit suicide one way or another, was gripped by a desire to pray. Snapping back to reality he knelt at his bedside and asked the Lord to come into his heart. He said, "Oh God, deliver me from this burden, I'll even preach!" He returned to his bed with a soothing peace settling over his mind and his future plans were settled. This was in the spring of 1875 when Torrey was 18 years old. In Yale chapel he made a public profession of faith and following graduation in 1875 he entered the Yale Divinity School.

Winning people to Christ became an obsession with him and soon he was renown as a great personal soul winner. After his conversion, the first time he saw the young lady he had been taking to dances, he witnessed to her. He says of the incident "...I commenced to reason with her out of the Scriptures. It took two hours but she accepted Christ."

Both of his parents died in the summer of 1877.

While in Seminary, Torrey first heard a man whom the students called a strange, uneducated evangelist. It was D. L. Moody at New Haven, Connecticut, in 1878. After Moody spoke, Torrey and others said, "Tell us how to win people to Jesus Christ." Moody said, "Go at it! That's the best way to learn!" So Torrey plunged into personal work starting right there at the meetings. His method was to put the Bible in the hands of the inquirer and have him read a selected passage. Torrey would then ask questions about the words and phrases of the passage until the seeker understood it. His approach to individuals was sometimes brusque and always direct and pointed. There was no attempt to try to win people to himself first as a means of winning them to Christ. It was always directly to Jesus Christ in his witnessing. Torrey also heard Moody say in another sermon, "Faith can do anything!" and faith became the keynote of his life. Reading the works of Finney those days also helped mold his life.

Torrey got his B.D. in 1878 with his D.D. coming later in 1889. He was ordained a Congregational minister in 1878 and pastored the Congregational Church in Garretsville, Ohio, a community of 1,000 from 1878 to 1882. It was during this time he married Clara Smith on October 22, 1879. His wife was a constant inspiration to him. They had five children beginning with Edith (November 8, 1880); Blanche, Reuben, Elizabeth and ending with Margaret (February 16, 1893).

Not satisfied with the training he received in the States, he studied at the German universities of Leipzig and Erlangen in 1882-83. As a brilliant student he made great progress in school. Early in his studies he was a pronounced higher critic but ere he had completed them, he was convinced of the falsity of his views and swung gradually back to old conservative doctrines, reversing the usual trend because of Europe's emphasis on higher criticism. In fact, Torrey became a most bitter foe of liberalism the rest of his days. He was hopelessly orthodox.

Upon returning to the states, he received two calls. One was to pastor a wealthy church in Brooklyn and the other to pastor a weak and poor church in Minneapolis, Minnesota. He chose the latter. He organized the church with about a dozen members and it became known as the Open Door Church. He stayed from 1883 to 1886 then moved on to the People's Church from 1887-89. Along with these pastoral responsibilities, he accepted the superintendency of

145

the Congregational City Mission Society, 1886-89. It was in Minneapolis that his motto became "pray through" as a result of reading Mueller's *Life of Trust*. He received no stated salary and was supported by free will offerings. He said later:

> A number of years ago (1888), I came to the place where it seemed my duty to give up my salary and work for God among the poor...From that day on, every mouthful came directly from my Heavenly Father, not a meal on our tables...not a coat that went on my back...not a dress on my wife's back, nor the clothing on the backs of our four children, that was not an answer to prayer. We got everything from God. I was never more serene in my life.

Mr. Torrey also made it a habit to hold special prayer meetings asking God to pour out His Spirit in mighty revival power around the world. Little did he suspect how instrumental his own life would be in bringing this to pass.

One day D. L. Moody was talking with a friend, E. M. Williams, and lamented that he wished he knew of a man to head his new school. Williams gave a glowing account of Torrey's ministries. Moody called for him and at the age of 33 Torrey became the first Superintendent of the Chicago Evangelization Society (later Moody Bible Institute), guiding it from its inception September 26, 1889, until 1908. He was the chief executive officer and the success of the Institute can probably be attributed to Torrey's contribution more than any other individual. He laid the ground work for the curriculum and the practical Christian work program. Torrey's leadership at the school, plus his part in the 1893 World's Fair evangelism outreach, brought him to the attention of the Christian world. Torrey was automatically considered the "Elisha" to carry on Moody's work upon his death in 1899. When Moody collapsed in Kansas City in November 1899 just prior to his death, it was Torrey who carried on the Crusade.

At school the students were constantly amazed at his ability. His teaching and prevailing prayer became renown. As he lectured in the classroom he poured out the brilliance of his Yale and German training, which had been endued with faith and emboldened by the Holy Spirit. He was sound in doctrine and an exceptional Bible teacher. His successor, James Gray, said of him, "Few men were better equipped than he to expound the Holy Scriptures before a popular audience or in a classroom." And how he could pray! One student reported how he went to Torrey's office with a particular need and after the session kneeling in prayer together was over a pool of tears remained when Torrey arose. His booklet *How to Pray* is a classic.

Torrey also took upon himself the pastorship of the Chicago Avenue Church (now Moody Memorial Church) from 1894 to 1905 where again he wielded a tremendous amount of influence in the Christian world. The 2,200 seat auditorium soon began to be filled. Torrey later said he didn't believe a day went by without someone being saved as a result of the church. The success was the prayer meetings, for all over the city there were little groups who would stay up late on Saturday night or get up early on Sunday morning to pray for their pastor. This, plus the fact that his membership was always trained in soul winning, produced a church that lived in a constant revival atmosphere. Every year he spent several months in Northfield, Massachusetts, teaching and preaching in the various conferences there.

In 1898 a weekly prayer meeting began at the Bible Institute each Saturday night from 9 to 10 p.m. The attendance grew until it numbered an average of 300 people. Its purpose was to pray for world-wide revival. For the next three years the prayer meetings continued followed by Torrey and three or four associates having a second prayer meeting until about 2 a.m. One night Torrey had a strange burden to pray that God would send him around the world with the Gospel. Within a week two strangers from the United Churches of Melbourne, Australia, approached him following a Sunday service saying they felt Torrey was the man God wanted to come to their country for evangelistic services. Torrey was stunned and challenged by the proposal. It seemed the years of praying were about to bear fruit.

Getting a leave of absence from his Chicago responsibilities, he quickly began to ponder that God might use him as the human instrument to bring world-wide revival...his burden for many years. He was to see some 102,000 come to Christ in the next few years in the most globe-girdling enterprise ever undertaken by an evangelist.

He wired a former student, Charles M. Alexander, to meet him in Australia. Torrey went to Japan and China on the way where he preached with great power and saw hundreds of converts made during his brief visit there.

It was April 1902 that Torrey and Alexander met in Melbourne, Australia, and began their work there. This movement was known at the Simultaneous Mission and it lasted a month. For the first two weeks meetings were held in fifty different centers by fifty different ministers and evangelists. The "Glory Song" (*O That Will Be Glory*) seemed to set the nation on fire. During the last two weeks the meetings were held in the Exhibition Building seating 8,000 people. Up to 15,000 were trying to get in nightly. W.E. Geil, another American evangelist, assisted in the meetings. Some 8,600 converts were recorded and the news of the awakening stirred all Christendom. Calls came from other key cities of Australia, Tasmania and New Zealand where they ministered for the next six months. In Sydney, Torrey spoke to thousands in the massive city hall with hundreds converted. In Bendigo, Alexander met and led Robert Harkness, a brilliant young musical genius, to Christ and he became his pianist soon joining the team for the rest of their tour. In one Australian city a largely built man thundered at Torrey, "I am not a Christian but I am moral, upright, honorable and blameless...and I'd like to know what you have against me!" Torrey looked him straight in the eyes and replied, "I charge you, sir, with high treason against Heaven's King!"

Up to 2,000 prayer bands were conducted in various sections of the country praying continually for revival.

Two campaigns were held in Tasmania, in Launceston and Hobart. The heavy-weight boxing champ of Tasmania confessed Christ as Savior the same night a member of Parliament did. Thirty days in New Zealand climaxed their tour. Revival fires broke out with a total of 20,000 decisions for Christ in the land "down under."

Calls now came from England and they headed that way stopping in India for six weeks enroute. Campaigns were held in Madura, Madras, Calcutta, Bombay and Benares. Hundreds were saved. A convention of 400 missionaries listened to Torrey for four days receiving much blessing to bring back to their people.

They were welcomed in London in a great meeting in Exeter Hall by the leading clerics of England. They spent three weeks in Mildmay Conference Hall in North London stirring up church members to fresh zeal in soul winning and witnessing, resulting in large numbers of conversions. They went on to Edinburgh, Scotland, for a four week campaign held in Synod Hall. In the weeks to follow they also ministered in France and Germany.

The team made a brief trip to America during July and August 1903 where a welcome home crowd of some 10,000 endeavored to gain admission to the Auditorium of the Bible Institute.

In September 1903 they were back in England and beginning the Liverpool crusade. In four weeks they saw about 5,000 converts. The crowds became so large that two meetings per night had to be held, one for women and the second for men. At Dublin, Ireland, at the Metropolitan Hall some 3,000 accepted Christ.

By 1904 some 30,000 persons around the world had committed themselves to pray for the team and world -wide revival. In January 1904 the Birmingham campaign began. It was probably the most successful campaign held anywhere on their tour. Meetings were held in Bingley Hall, seating 8,000 with space for 2,000 standees. The thirty day crusade had some 7,000 conversions! Here Alexander met his future wife, Helen Cadbury, whom he married in July.

In September 1904 the team was in Bolton, Wales (3,600 saved), then on to Cardiff to a 7,000 seat auditorium which filled nightly (3,750 saved). Evan Roberts led that nation to God the next year and surely the sparks of revival were lit at those meetings.

From Cardiff the evangelists went back to Liverpool to conduct a nine week campaign. The Tournament Hall, seating 12,500 was reserved. At times it proved inadequate and it is estimated some 35,000 were turned away on the last day of the meetings. Some 7,000 were saved and an old resident said it surpassed the Moody-Sankey revival many years previously. The choir numbered 3,658 alone which was the largest evangelistic chorus ever organized up to that time. Two banquets were held averaging 2,200 each for the poor people of Liverpool averaging about 225 decisions for Christ at each.

From February to June 1905 the famous London Crusade was held. Total expenses amounted to $85,000 with nearly 15,000 professed conversions. Meetings were held at the Royal Albert Hall for the first two months; an iron and glass building seating 5,500 in South London for the next two months and another great iron building seating over 5,000 in the heart of London on the Strand for the last month. A 1,000 voice choir helped nightly. The crusade began at the 11,000 seat Royal Albert Hall on February 4 with a welcome by many of the city's dignitaries. The first evangelistic service was held the following night with 10,000 unable to secure admission. Some 250 were saved. A well known concert hall singer and entertainer by the name of Quentin Ashlyn was saved soon after. It seemed as though all of London was singing revival hymns. The *"Glory Song"* captured the city. It was sung at every service. *Tell Mother I'll Be There* was also greatly used. Some 6,500 were saved at the Royal Albert Hall with special meetings for men and children also packing out the hall. Meetings held in South London produced 5,000 converts and then in the final month another 2,500 were saved. A closing service at the Royal Albert Hall announced the totals...202 meetings, 1,114,650 attended (average 5,500 per service) with over 17,000 converts!

Wherever they had gone...to Glasgow, Edinburg, Aberdeen or Dundee in Scotland to Dublin and Belfast in Ireland (4,000 saved) to Manchester (4,000 saved) and the other above mentioned crusades in England and Wales, the halls were unable to hold the crowds. Not since the days of Moody and Sankey had Great Britain been so stirred. A total of 70,000 came to the Lord during these three years of ministry there.

Returning to the United States in December 1905 with more revival preaching on his mind, he made his leave of absence permanent at the two hallowed institutions that had stood by awaiting his return. James M. Gray became the chief executive officer at Moody Bible Institute and A.C. Dixon became pastor of Moody Church. From 1906 to 1911 a heavy series of crusades in America occupied his time Oswald J. Smith was converted in the 1906 Toronto, Ontario, crusade. Atlanta, Ottawa, Ontario, San Francisco, Omaha, Cleveland, Nashville, Buffalo, Montreal, Quebec, Detroit, Los Angeles and Chicago all had good revival sessions with him. Perhaps his most successful revival stateside was in Philadelphia in the spring of 1906. Newspaper headlines blared out, "Hell is absolutely certain, Dr. Torrey warns his hearers!" These meetings lasted 62 days in three different armories at a cost of $38,365. John Wanamaker and John Converse, successful Christian businessmen, were among the chief supporters. Some 7,000 converts were claimed, although decision cards totaled only 3,615. Charles Alexander left Torrey in 1907-08 and joined up with J. Wilbur Chapman.

Torrey helped establish the Montrose (Pennsylvania) Bible Conference in 1908. Later he would be buried there on Conference Hill.

In 1911 he went back to England, Scotland and Ireland for more meetings.

Now a call came from the West Coast to give Los Angeles similar institutions to those he led in Chicago. From 1912 to 1924 he served as Dean of the Los Angeles Bible Institute (now called BIOLA). He also helped to organize and served as the first pastor of the Church of the Open Door (1915-1924). There he preached to great throngs and God blessed both his pastoring and teaching. Thousands were trained at the school including Charles E. Fuller, famed radio preacher of the next generation.

In 1919 he visited Japan and China with the Gospel and in 1921 he toured China and Korea in evangelistic endeavors.

From 1924 to 1928 he devoted his time to holding Bible conferences, giving special lectures at the Moody Bible Institute among other places. He made his home in Biltmore, North Carolina. He passed on quietly at Asheville, North Carolina.

Will Houghton, preaching his funeral said:

...But those who knew Dr. Torrey more intimately knew him as a man of regular and uninterrupted prayer. He knew what it meant to pray without ceasing. With hours set systematically apart for prayer, he gave himself diligently to this ministry.

Reuben A. Torrey wrote some forty books and his practical writings on the Holy Spirit, prayer, salvation, soul winning and evangelism are still favorites of many Christians. His *Gist of the Lesson* continued for more than thirty years. This was a series of helps on the International Sunday School lessons. Many of his works have been translated into foreign languages.

His first book was *How To Bring Men To Christ* (1893). His last, *Lectures On The First Epistle Of John*, published in 1929 after his death. His *How To Promote and Conduct A Successful Revival* (1901) is considered one of the best books on personal and mass evangelism ever written.

The Life
And Ministry Of

John Benjamin Wesley
1703 ~ 1791

JOHN BENJAMIN WESLEY

BORN: June 17, 1703
Epworth, England

DIED: March 2, 1791
London, England

LIFE SPAN: 87 years, 8 months, 13 days

John Wesley was perhaps the busiest man who ever lived in the service of the Lord. He traveled almost constantly, mostly on horseback (average 15-20 miles per day), preaching two or three times a day. He formed societies, opened chapels for services, examined and commissioned preachers, administered discipline, raised funds for schools, chapels and charities, prescribed help for the sick, superintended schools and orphanages, prepared commentaries and a vast amount of other Christian literature, defended Methodism from attacks, engaged in numerous controversies, carried on a huge correspondence and oversaw everything as Methodism developed. In his life time he traveled over 250,000 miles on horseback, preached about 42,000 times, wrote, translated or edited some 233 volumes of sermons, commentaries, hymns and the *Christian Library* of 50 volumes. He authored 30 books. His *Journal* began October 14, 1735, and continued for 55 years to October 24, 1790. It is referred to by some as the most amazing record of human exertion ever penned by man. He arose at 4 A.M., lived simply and methodically and was never idle. He had a poor marriage with no children and was seldom at home. When he died there were some 118,000 to 153,000 Methodists, over 500 itinerant preachers whom he had ordained, some 214 church circuits and the Methodist denomination which has grown to one of the largest in the world. Little did he realize how prophetic his statement became, "The world is my parish."

He was the 15th child of Samuel and Susanna Wesley whose total off-spring numbered 19. Only ten of these survived infancy. The training of his mother was especially important to these children and her fame as a Christian mother and wife has long been known. On February 7, 1709, a near tragedy occurred when the parsonage caught fire. The children (8 living) had a narrow escape with John, almost six, being pulled out of an upper window by neighbors as the house was about to cave in. His mother said that he was "a brand plucked from the burning." Susanna spent time with John every Thursday night.

Wesley was educated at the Charterhouse School in London from January 28, 1713, to 1720. He lived the studious, methodical and religious life in which he had been trained. On June 24, 1720, he went up to Christ Church, Lincoln College, Oxford, with an annual allowance as a Charterhouse scholar. His health was poor but he made good use of his opportunities. During this time he studied the writings of Kempis and Jeremy Taylor. He received a B.A. degree here at Oxford in 1724. On September 19, 1725, he was ordained a deacon in the Church of England. He preached his first sermon in South Leigh. On March 17, 1726, he was made a fellow of Lincoln College, Oxford. He preached frequently in the churches near Oxford in the months following his ordination and in April 1726 obtained leave from his college to act as his father's assistant. In October 1726, he returned to Oxford where he was appointed Greek lecturer and moderator of the classics. He received his Masters Degree on February 14, 1727. On August 4, 1727, he returned to Epworth where he assisted his father, an Anglican pastor, until November 22, 1729. During this time he was ordained a priest in the Anglican (Church of England) Church on September 22, 1728, by John Potter. Also, he kept in touch with his university making three visits, including a two month trek in the summer of 1729. Evenings there were spent with the little society that was gathering around his brother Charles, including George Whitefield.

In November 1729 he went back to the residence at Oxford and soon became the recognized leader of the "Holy Club." He returned to fulfill duties as fellow and moderator. Meeting first only on Sunday evenings it soon became an evening gathering in someone's room where they read the Greek New Testament and classics, fasted on Wednesdays and Fridays, received the Lord's Supper weekly and brought all their life under review. They had an opportunity to visit the prisoners in the Castle twice a week and also began to look after the sick in any parish where the clergyman was willing to accept their help. Because of their methodical ministries and devotion to Christ, they were dubbed Methodists. Wesley did not like the name but adopted it as a badge of honor and proceeded to define it as meaning an authentic Christian. Wesley's duties while at Lincoln College, Oxford, from 1729 to 1735, were serving as tutor, moderator for logic classes, Greek New Testament lecturer and claviger (keeper of the keys). A University sermon preached by Wesley on January 1, 1733, entitled *The Circumcision of the Heart*, portrayed his feelings...the quest for holiness which was to follow him the rest of his life. Concerning these years, Wesley reported that from 1725 to 1729 he saw no fruit, 1729 to 1734 -- little fruit and from 1734 to 1738 -- more fruit in his preaching. Then in 1738 he was converted! But we are ahead of our story.

Wesley's father died on April 25, 1735. On October 14 he, his brother Charles and two others went to America to work amongst the Indians. They did not sail until December 10. General Oglethorpe in Georgia had requested a clergyman. They were sent out by the Society for the Propagation of the Gospel but the trip was not a success. However, an experience on the way over was worth the trip. A severe storm (January 25) buffeted the boat and brought great fear into the hearts of the Wesleys. On board for Georgia as well, a group of 21 German Moravians were composed as they sang a psalm. The next day the Moravian pastor, Spargenberg, had a question for Wesley..."Friend, Wesley, do you know Jesus Christ?" "I know that He is the Saviour of the world," was the reply. The Moravian countered, "But can you tell me if He has saved you?" Wesley meekly replied, "I hope so." He was later to wail. "I came to Georgia to convert the Indians, but, oh, who shall convert me? I have but a fair summer religion!" They arrived at Savannah, February 6, 1736. Lack of salvation was not the only reason Wesley's ministry failed in America. He was a high-churchman. His views were strict and censorious and his refusal to administer communion to Miss Sophy Hopkey, after she became Mrs. Williamson, was unfortunate in view of the courtship that had existed between them before her marriage. He had interesting conversation with the Indians but failed in converting them. In Savannah, Georgia, where he ministered for the most part, the German Moravian friends deepened his impression that all was not well with his soul. Charles Wesley returned within one year. John stayed on and in April 1736 did form a small group of about 35 that met as a congregation--meeting in Savannah every Wednesday night for conversation, singing and prayers. This was his only stint at pastoring and the rudiments of Methodism may have been born there. He left December 22, 1737, after his only visit to America. He did learn German on his voyage over enabling him to translate German hymns into English.

He arrived back in England on February 1, 1738, and made several unsuccessful attempts at preaching. On May 1, 1738, just prior to his conversion he wrote in his journal, "This evening our little society began." The society divided up into small bands of people (five or ten) who spoke freely and plainly to each other about their heart's condition. The bands united in a conference every Wednesday night. This was a Moravian project. Wesley had been interested in them ever since his journey across the Atlantic and had searched them out in London. Peter Bohler, Moravian leader, had been counseling with John's brother Charles and conversed with John about spiritual things beginning February 7. He invited John to a Christian society meeting on Aldersgate Street at a place called St. Paul's.

It was Wednesday, May 24, 1738. At 5 A.M. Wesley opened up his New Testament and meditated on II Peter 1:4. That evening he went, rather unwillingly, to the above mentioned meeting where *Luther's Preface to the Epistle to the Romans* was being read. His famous testimony tells what happened:

> About a quarter before nine, while he was describing the
> change which God works in the heart through faith in Christ,
> I felt my heart strangely warmed. I felt I *did* trust in Christ,
> Christ alone, for salvation; and an assurance was given me
> that He had taken away my sins, even mine, and saved me
> from the law of sin and death!

He rushed home to tell his brother Charles who had been converted four days previously and Charles suggested they sing a hymn together that he had just written the day before, *Christ the Friend of Sinners*.

Eighteen days later (June 11), Wesley preached at the University of Oxford, a long remembered sermon, *"By Grace are ye Saved through Faith."* He spent some time during June leaving the 13th, traveling to the Moravian settlement at Herrnhut (Germany), returning to London on September 16, 1738, with his faith greatly encouraged. Zinzendorf and the Moravians were a blessing to him, but he did not feel their plan of separate towns was a proper one. John felt that Christians should not withdraw from the world but work in it. He set out "to reform the nation, particularly the Church and to spread scriptural holiness over the land." He began to preach in all the churches that were open to him (and soon there were not too many) plus holding services at

Newgate and Oxford prisons.

About September 25, the weekly united meeting of the various Moravian bands was moved to Fetter Lane; they previously met in a shop. On November 5, the title "leader" was given to each of those who had charge of the London bands. The leaders soon became a body of lay pastors. Those under their care formed a class. Meeting together gave them an opportunity for conversation and prayer. Wesley published a book of hymns for them. As the work progressed, many faithful co-workers came on the scene. His first lay preacher was Joseph Humphreys (1738) followed by John Cennick (1729) and Thomas Maxwell who was left to meet with members at the Foundry during the Wesleys' absence. By 1741 lay preachers were a vital part of the ever expanding work of John Wesley.

On January 1, 1739, the Wesleys, Whitefield and others had a Love Feast at Fetter Lane following a watch-night prayer meeting. In February Whitefield began his field preaching. Wesley felt this was not proper, but seeing the results Whitefield was getting, he too began to preach in the fields on April 12, 1739. His first sermon in the open air was preached near Bristol to 3,000 mill workers. He was to spend the next 50 years in field-preaching. He entered churches when he was invited but took his stand in the fields, in halls, cottages and chapels when the churches would not receive him. In May 1739 Wesley's headquarters at Bristol were in the Horse Fair where a room was built for two religious societies. This was the first Methodist chapel erected. As his field preaching increased the number of converts, he invited the "new babes" to meet with him on Thursday evenings. On November 11, 1739, with cold weather coming, services were held in an abandoned foundry in Moorsfield (London) which Wesley had secured for a second preaching place. On July 23, 1740, Wesley withdrew from the Moravian society at Fetter Lane because of grave differences. He felt they had fallen into heresies, especially quietism, and so his followers (some 73 that came with him) formed a separate society. Thus began the Methodist Society in England and, in a sense, Methodism was born. Similar societies were soon formed in Bristol and Kingswood and wherever Wesley and his associates made converts.

The doctrine of election had led to a temporary separation of Whitefield and the Wesleys in 1742. His journal speaks of divine healing on May 10, 1741. Wesley believed that the grace of God could transform every life that received it. He preached daily growth in holiness. "Victory over sin should be the goal of every Christian," he thundered. Wesley had a mastery over his audiences. His Armenian doctrine is set forth in his four volumes of sermons and his *Notes on the New Testaments* in January 1750. The two men were later reconciled. Wesley preached his memorial November 18, 1770, at the Tabernacle Moorfields.

Up until 1742 Wesley's work was confined basically to Bristol and London and places in between. In May 1742, the work was extended into the north of England and on his way to Newcastle-upon-Tyne he visited Bristol. Upon his return, he held a memorable service in the churchyard at Epworth, June 6, 1742, being refused an opportunity to preach in his father's former parish. He went instead to the tombstone of his father in the churchyard and preached to thousands there. He did this again January 2, 1743. Societies (out-growth of classes) were now beginning to form in many cities and areas. His mother died July 23, 1742, John with her at the time. A visit to Cornwall in late August 1743 was very successful. Thousands were now hearing Wesley as he traveled from place to place even at 5 A.M. His 30,000 (largest audience) was August 21, 1773, when he was 70--at Gwennap. He was occasionally hustled and once or twice had mud, eggs and stones pelt him. Once he was pushed off a high wall.

From 1742 on the class-meeting system continued to grow. He resolved to visit each society once in three months. Thus arose the quarterly conference. As the societies increased, he could not continue his practice of oral instruction; so in February 1743 he drew up a set of "General Rules" for the "United Societies" which included a regenerated membership ("a desire to flee from the wrath to come, to be saved from their sins"). This became the nucleus of the *Methodist Discipline*, and is still preserved intact and observed by some Methodist bodies. As the number of preacher and preaching-places increased, it became desirable that doctrinal matters should be discussed, difficulties solved, distribution of the fields defined and other expansion problems resolved. Hence the two Wesleys with four other clergymen and four lay preachers met for consultation in London on June 25, 1744. This was the first Methodist conference and began the practice of preachers coming to him. This ultimately became the cornerstone of the governmental system of the Methodist Church. It was decided here that lay assistants were allowable, but only in cases of necessity. However the necessities became more urgent each year as the work spread and grew. One of the preachers in each circuit was the assistant who had general oversight of the work, all others were helpers. This conference then became an annual gathering of Wesley's preachers (or assistants). Things began to improve; societies had regular services; Wesley appointed "helpers" to definite circuits, each of which included at least 30 appointments per month. Realizing that many of his assistants and helpers were uneducated and finished their usefulness in a short time, the workers were switched often. He believed their usefulness and efficiency were prompted by being changed from one circuit to another every year or two, so he established itineraries and insisted that his preachers should submit to these rules. He was a bit dictatorial in this but, like William Booth of the Salvation Army later, someone had to lead and Wesley's vast organizational skills developed the movement. The breach between Wesley and the Church of England grew wider as his societies multiplied. In 1745 he wrote that he would make any concession his conscience would permit to remain in good graces with the established clergy but he could not give up the doctrine of salvation by faith alone, nor cease to preach in private houses and the open air, nor dissolve existing societies. In 1748 he started a boarding school at Kings Wood for children.

His ordination of preachers simply amounted to his appointing them to a certain field. It was not until many years later (1784) that he ordained with the laying on of hands. By 1746 he had pretty well mapped out the major features of Methodism. In August 1747 he paid his first visit to Ireland, where he had so much success that he gave more than six years of his life to this country crossing the Irish Channel 42 times. Wesley's first visit to Scotland was in 1751. In all he visited there 22 times. In 1775 he went back to both countries for an important series of meetings. In 1783 he visited Holland. Despite his unswerving loyalty to the Church of England, some of his preachers began to agitate as early at 1750 for ministerial standing and "separation" from the Establishment. They were labeled nonconformists.

On February 18, (age 48) 1751, he married a widow, Mary Vazeille, but the union was unfortunate and she finally left him 20 years later when he was 73 years of age (1776). She died in 1781. Wesley had almost married happily in 1748 to a Grace Murray.

The breach over Armenian theology broke out afresh in 1770 with Wesley and John Fletcher on one side and the Church of England leaders, Toplady, Berridge, Rowland and Hill, on the other side, although Wesley conducted the Whitefield Memorial Services of that year. Fletcher joined with Wesley in 1757 and was his closest friend until his death in 1782. In 1778 Wesley began the publication of *The Armenian Magazine*, which was to preserve Methodism more than to convert Calvinists. In 1780 it was known as the *Methodist Magazine*. In June 1775 he had a sickness nigh unto death. In November 1778 he preached the first sermon in the City Road Chapel.

In February 1784 Wesley did a wise thing. He filed a Deed of Declaration with the Court of Chancery of Great Britain. The "Conference" was given full legal status, its membership defined and its authority to appoint, control and expel preachers was asserted. Listed were 359 ministers. This made Methodists self-governing and self-perpetuating and gives us a sample of Wesley's organizational skills. He also named 100 preachers who, after his death, were to meet once a year, fill vacancies in their number, appoint a president and secretary, station the preachers, admit proper persons into the ministry and take general oversight of the societies.

In 1780 Wesley had asked the bishop of London to ordain a minister for the American Methodists (began 1766) but he declined. So the final breach with the Church of England came on September 13, 1784, when at Bristol Wesley ordained Richard Whatcoat and Thomas Vasey for the American ministry and consecrated Thomas Coke, already a priest of the Church of England, as "superintendent" for the same work -- a title which was soon transformed in America, apparently by Coke himself, into that of "bishop." He also ordained Alexander Mather at this time for work in England and stated that both Coke and Mather would be free to ordain others. Coke in turn ordained Francis Asbury and Methodism was off to a running start in America. Methodism was now providing its own self-perpetuating ministry and the breach with the Church of England was complete. Rejoicing that his American followers were free from entanglements with Church and State, he counseled his English followers to remain in the established Church, and he himself died in the Anglican communion. He had simply considered Methodism as an evangelistic extension of the Church of England. However, the feelings were not as charitable from the Church and they did everything possible to disassociate themselves from Wesley. One year later Wesley ordained several others of his preachers, "to administer the sacraments of baptism and the Lord's Supper, according to the usage of the Church of England," in such places as Scotland and Ireland as well as England.

His writings, as mentioned earlier, were numerous. He published his *Collected Works* in 32 volumes. He felt free to reprint, abridge, or digest the writings of others or to produce his own, according to the circumstances. The bulk of his publications concern his revival ministry and the progress of the new movement -- the *Journal*, the *Sermons*, the *Hymns*, the *Appeals*, the *Plain Account of Christian Perfection*, the *Explanatory Notes on the New Testament* and his *Appeals to Men of Reason and Religion*. As already stated *The Journal of John Wesley* is about as extensive a biography as is available. He provided people with textbooks of various sorts, with histories, political commentaries and a medical handbook called *Primitive Physick*. He pioneered in most of the good causes of his day; legal and prison reform, the abolition of slavery which he detested (1772 -- "that execrable scum of all villainies"), civil rights, popular education and the encouragement of the Sunday school movement. His sermon *"The Great Assize"* was a classic. He preached in German, French and Italian and could read Hebrew, Greek and Latin and could pray in Spanish.

Fletcher's death in 1785 and that of Charles Wesley in 1788 were big losses to him. Once at 84 he traveled 240 miles in 80 hours. During his last three years of life he was welcomed everywhere. His visits became public holidays. He caught a cold February 17 and preached his last sermon in Mr. Belson's home at Leatherhead on Wednesday, February 23, 1791; wrote his last letter the next day -- to Wilberforce, urging him to carry on his crusade against the slave trade -- and then died in his house on City Road on March 2 after a short illness.

The soldier died with great confidence, saying such things as "The best of all is, God is with us" "The Lord is with us, the God of Jacob is our refuge," during his last days. His last night heard him trying to repeat a Psalm but he could only get out, "I'll Praise -- I'll Praise." On Wednesday morning his last word was "Farewell," and with friends kneeling around his bed, he was gone. Services were held March 9 by Mr. Richards an itinerant preacher of Wesley's for over 30 years and a Dr. Whitehead who preached. He was buried in the graveyard behind City Road Chapel. He was 5' 5" tall and weighed 122 pounds. The verse that gave him the most comfort was Mark 12:34.

The Life
And Ministry Of

George Whitefield
1714 ~ 1770

GEORGE WHITEFIELD

BORN: December 16, 1714   **DIED:** September 30, 1770
Gloucester, England   Newburyport, Massachusetts
LIFE SPAN: 55 years, 9 months, 14 days

Whitefield was the most traveled preacher of the gospel up to his time and many feel he was the greatest evangelist of all time. Making 13 trips across the Atlantic Ocean was a feat in itself, for it was during a time when sea travel was primitive. This meant he spent over two years of his life traveling on water - 782 days. However, his diligence and sacrifice helped turn two nations back to God. Jonathan Edwards was stirring up things in New England and John Wesley was doing the same in England. Whitefield completed the trio of men humanly responsible for the great awakening on both sides of the Atlantic. He spent about 24 years of ministry in the British Isles and about nine more years in America speaking to some ten million souls.

It is said that his voice could be heard a mile away and his open air preaching reached as many as 100,000 in one gathering! His crowds were the greatest ever assembled to hear the preaching of the gospel before the days of amplification...and if we might add, before the days of advertising.

He was born in the Bell Inn where his father, Thomas, was a wine merchant and innkeeper. The father died when George was two. George was the youngest of seven children. His widowed mother, Elizabeth (born 1680) struggled to keep the family together. When the lad was about ten his mother remarried but it was not a happy union. Childhood measles left him squint-eyed the rest of his life. When he was twelve he was sent to the St. Mary de Crypt Grammar School in Gloucester. There he had a record of truancy but also a reputation as an actor and orator.

About 15 years of age he persuaded his mother to let him leave school because he would never make much use of his education...so he thought! He spent time working in the inn.

Hidden in the back of his mind was a desire to preach. At night George sat up and read the Bible. Mother was visited by an Oxford student who worked his way through college and this report encouraged both mother and George to plan for college. He returned to grammar school to finish his preparation to enter Oxford losing about one year of school.

When he was 17 he entered Pembroke College at Oxford in November 1732. He was gradually drawn from former sinful associates and after a year met John and Charles Wesley and joined the Holy Club. Charles Wesley loaned him a book, *The Life of God in the Soul of Man*. This book plus a severe sickness which resulted because of long and painful periods of spiritual struggle finally resulted in his conversion. This was in 1735. He said many years later:

> I know the place...Whenever I go to Oxford, I cannot help running to the spot where Jesus Christ first revealed Himself to me, and gave me the new birth.

160

Many days and weeks of fasting and all the other tortures to which he had exposed himself so undermined his health that he was never again a well man. Because of poor health, he left school in May 1735 and returned home for nine months of recuperation. However, he was far from idle and his activity attracted the attention of Dr. Benson who was the bishop of Gloucester. He announced he would gladly ordain Whitefield as a deacon. Whitefield returned to Oxford in March of 1736 and on June 20, 1736, Bishop Benson ordained him. He placed his hands upon his head whereupon George later declared, "My heart was melted down, and I offered my whole spirit, soul and body to the service of God's sanctuary."

Whitefield preached his first sermon the following Sunday. It was at the ancient Church of Saint Mary de Crypt, the church where he had been "baptized" and grown up as a boy. People, including his mother, flocked to hear him. He describes it later:

> ...Some few mocked, but most for the present, seemed struck, and I have since heard that a complaint was made to the bishop, that I drove fifteen people mad, the first sermon.

Eighteen thousand sermons were to follow in his lifetime, an average of 500 a year or ten a week. Many of them were given over and over again. Less than 90 of them have survived in any form.

The Wednesday following his first sermon he returned to Oxford where the B.A. degree was conferred upon him. Then he was called to London to act as a supply minister at the Tower of London. He stayed only a couple of months and then returned to Oxford for a very short time, helping a friend in a rural parish for a few weeks. He also spent much time amongst the prisoners at Oxford during this time.

The Wesley brothers had gone to Georgia and Whitefield got letters from them urging him to come there. He felt called to go but the Lord delayed the trip for a year, during which time he began to preach with power to great crowds throughout London and soon no church was large enough to hold those who came to hear him.

He finally left for America from England on January 10 and on February 2, 1738, sailed from Gibraltar, although he had left England in December. The boat was delayed a couple of places but Whitefield used the extra time preaching. He arrived in America on May 7, 1738. Shortly after arrival he had a severe bout with a fever. Upon recovering he visited Tomo -Chici, Indian king, who was on his death bed. With no interpreter, Whitefield could only offer a prayer in his behalf. He loved Georgia and was not discouraged here as were the Wesleys. He was burdened about orphans and started to collect funds for the same. He opened schools in Highgate and Hampstead and also a school for girls in Savannah. Of course he also preached. On September 9, 1738, he left Charleston, South Carolina, for the trip back to London. It was a perilous voyage. For two weeks a bad storm beat the boat. About one-third of the way home they met a ship from Jamaica which had ample supplies to restock the dwindling food and water cargo on their boat. After nine weeks of tossing to and fro, they found themselves in the harbor of Limerick, Ireland, and in

London in December.

On Sunday, January 14, 1739, he was ordained as a priest in the church of England by his friend Bishop Benson in an Oxford ceremony.

Upon his return he thought that the doors would be opened and that he would be warmly received. Instead it was the opposite. Now many churches were closed to him. His successes, preaching and connection with the Methodist societies were all opposed by the establishment. However, he preached to as many churches as would receive him, working and visiting with such as the Moravians and other non-conformist religious societies in London. However, these buildings were becoming too small to hold the crowds. Alternative plans had to be formulated.

Howell Harris of Wales was preaching in the fields. Whitefield wondered if he ought to try it too. He concluded he was an outcast anyway so why not try to reach people this "new" way? He held a conference with the Wesleys and other Oxford Methodists before going to Bristol in February. Soon Wesley would be forced to follow Whitefield's example.

Just outside the city of Bristol was a coal mine district known as Kingswood Hill. Whitefield first preached here in the open on February 17, 1739. The first time about 200 came to hear him, but in a very short time he was preaching to 10,000 at once. Often they stood in the rain listening with the melodies of their singing being heard two miles away.

One of his favorite preaching places was just outside London on a great open tract known as Moorfields. He had no designated time for his services, but whenever he began to preach thousands came to hear whether it was 6 a.m. or 8 p.m. Not all were fans as evidenced by his oft repeated testimony, "I was honored with having stones, dirt, rotten eggs and pieces of dead cats thrown at me." In the morning some 20,000 listened to him and in the evening some 35,000 gathered! Whitefield was only 25 years old. Crowds up to 80,000 at one time gathered there to hear him preach for $1^{1}/_{2}$ hours.

There seems to be nothing unusual in content about his printed sermons but his oratory put great life into them. He could paint word pictures with such breathless vividness that crowds listening would stare through tear-filled eyes as he spoke. Once while describing an old man trembling toward the edge of a precipice, Lord Chesterfield jumped to his feet and shouted as George walked the man unknowingly toward the edge, "He is gone." Another time in Boston he described a storm at sea. There were many sailors in the crowd and at the very height of the tempest an old salt jumped to his feet and shouted, "To the lifeboats, men, to the lifeboats!" Often as high as 500 would fall in the group and lay prostrate under the power of a single sermon. Many people made demonstrations and in several instances men who held out against the Spirit's wooing dropped dead during his meetings. Audible cries of the audience often interrupted the messages. People usually were saved right during the progress of the service. The altar call as such was not utilized.

On August 1, 1739, the Bishop of London denounced him, nevertheless on August 14 he was on his way to his second trip to America taking with him about $4,000 which he had raised for his orphanage. This time he landed near

Philadelphia on October 30, preaching here before going south. The old courthouse had a balcony and Whitefield loved to preach from it whenever he came here. People stood in the streets all around to listen to him. When preaching on Society Hill near Philadelphia, he spoke to 6,000 in the morning and 8,000 in the evening. On the following Sunday the respective crowds were 10,000 to 25,000. At a farewell address more than 35,000 gathered to hear him. Benjamin Franklin became a good friend of the evangelist and was always impressed, although not converted. Once Franklin emptied his pockets at home knowing that an offering would be taken. So powerful was the appeal that he ended up borrowing money from a stranger sitting nearby.

From Philadelphia, Whitefield went to New York. Again the people thronged to hear him by the thousands. He preached to 8,000 in the field on Sunday mornings to 15,000 and Sunday afternoon to 20,000. He returned again and again to these cities.

After a short stay here, he was eager to reach Georgia. He went by land with at least 1,000 people accompanying him from Philadelphia to Chester. Here he preached to thousands with even the judges postponing their business until his sermon was over. He preached at various places journeying through Maryland and ending up at Chesterton, South Carolina. He finally ended up in Savannah on January 10, 1740, going by canoe from Charleston. His first order of business was to get an orphanage started. He rented a large house for a temporary habitation for the homeless waifs and on March 25, 1740, he laid the first brick of the main building which he named Bethesda, meaning house of mercy.

With things under control in the south, he sailed up to New England in September of 1740 for his first of three trips to that area. He arrived at Newport, Rhode Island, to commence what historians call the focal point of "the first great awakening." Edwards had been sowing the seed throughout the area -- and Whitefield's presence was the straw to break the devil's back. He preached in Boston to the greatest crowds ever assembled there to hear the Gospel. Some 8,000 assembled in the morning and some 15,000 returned to the famous Commons in the evening. At Old North Church thousands were turned away so he took his message outside to them. Later Governor Belcher drove him to the Common where 20,000 were waiting to hear him. He was invited more than once to speak to the faculty and students of Harvard. At Salem, hundreds could not get into the building where he spoke.

He then preached four times for Edwards in Northampton, Massachusetts (October 17-20), and though he stayed in New England less than a month that time--the revival that was started lasted for a year and a half. He left January 24, 1741, and returned to England March 14, 1741; he found that Wesley was diverging from Calvinist doctrine, so he withdrew from the Wesley Connection which he had embraced. Thereupon his friends built him a wooden church named the Moorfields Tabernacle. A reconciliation was made between the two evangelists but they both went their separate ways. From this time on Whitefield was considered the unofficial leader of Calvinistic Methodism.

Unique details are available following his break with Wesley. They begin with his first of fourteen trips to Scotland on July 30, 1741. This trip was sponsored by the Seceders but he refused to limit his ministrations to this one sect who had invited him, so he broke with them. Continuing his tour, he was received everywhere with enthusiasm. In Glasgow many were brought under deep conviction. The largest audience he ever addressed was at Cambuslang near Glasgow where he spoke to an estimated 100,000 people! He preached for $1^1/_2$ hours to the tearful crowd. Converts from that one meeting numbered nearly 10,000. Once he preached to 30,000; another day he had five services of 20,000. Then he went on to Edinburg where he preached to 10,000 souls every day. He loved it so much he cried out, "May I die preaching" which in essence, he did.

Then he went on to Wales where he was to make frequent trips in the future and was received with great respect and honor. Here he met his wife to be, Elizabeth James, an older widow. They were married there on November 14, 1741, and on October 4, 1743, one son was born named John who died at age four months the following February.

In 1742 a second trip was made to Scotland. During the first two visits here Scotland was spiritually awakened and set "on fire" as she had not been since the days of John Knox. Subsequent visits did not evidence the great revivals of the early trips, but these were always refreshing times for the people. Then a tour through England and Wales was made from 1742-1744. It was in 1743 that he began as moderator for the Calvinistic Methodists in Wales, which position he held a number of years.

In 1744 he almost became a martyr. A man uttering abusive language, called him a dog, villain and so forth, proceeded to beat him unmercifully with a gold headed cane until he was almost unconcious. He was also accused of misappropriating funds which he had collected. Nothing could be further from the truth.

At least once he had to sell what earthly possessions he had in order to pay a certain debt that he had incurred for his orphanage, and to give his aged mother the things she needed. Friends had loaned him the furniture that he needed when he lived in England. When he died he was a pauper with only a few personal possessions being the extent of his material gain.

Another trip was made to America from 1744 to 1748. On his way home because of ill health, he visited the Bermudas. It was a pleasant trip where he preached regularly and saw many souls won to the Lord. It was in 1748 that he said, "Let the name of Whitefield die so that the cause of Christ may live." A fourth trip to America was made October 27, 1751 to May 1752.

Upon his return to England he was appointed one of the chaplains to Selina, Countess of Huntingdon--known as Lady Huntingdon, a friend since 1748. His mother died at age 71 in December of 1751. In 1753 he compiled "Hymns for Social Worship." This was also the year he traveled 800 miles on horseback preaching to 10,000 souls. It was during this time that he was struck on the head by stones and knocked off a table upon which he had been preaching. Afterwards he said, "We are immortal till our work is done," a phrase he would often repeat.

In 1754 Whitefield embarked again for America with 22 orphans. Enroute he visited Lisbon, Portugal, and spent four weeks there. In Boston thousands waited for his preaching at 7 a.m. One auditorium seating 4,000 saw great numbers turned away while Whitefield, himself, had to be helped in through a window. He stayed from May 1753 to May 1755

In 1756 he was in Ireland. He made only two, possibly three trips here. On this occasion (age 42) he almost met death. On Sunday afternoon while preaching on a beautiful green field near Dublin, stones and dirt were hurled at him. Afterwards a mob gathered intending to take his life. Those attending to him fled and he was left to walk nearly a half a mile alone, while rioters threw great showers of stones upon him from every direction until he was covered with blood. He staggered to the door of a minister living close by. Later he said, "I received many blows and wounds; one was particularly large near my temples." He later said that in Ireland he had been elevated to the rank of an Apostle in having had the honor of being stoned. Also in 1756 he opened the Congregational chapel bearing his name on Tottenham Court Road, London. He ministered here and at the before-mentioned Moorsfield Tabernacle often. A sixth trip was made to America in 1763-1765.

In 1768 he made his last trip to Scotland 27 years after his first. He was forced to conclude, "I am here only in danger of being hugged to death." He visited Holland where he sought help for his body, where his health did improve. It is also recorded that he once visited Spain. His wife died on August 9, 1768, and Whitefield preached the funeral sermon using Romans 8:28 as a text. He dedicated the famous Tottenham Court Road Chapel on July 23, 1769.

On September 4, 1769, he started on his last voyage to America, arriving November 30. He went on business to make arrangements for his orphanage to be converted into Bethesda College. He spent the winter months of 1769-70 in Georgia, then with the coming of spring he started north. He arrived in Philadelphia in May traveling on to New England. Never was he so warmly received as now. The crowds flocked to see him in great numbers. July was spent preaching in New York and Albany and places enroute. In August he reached Boston. For three days in September he was too ill to preach, but as soon as he could be out of bed he was back preaching. His last letter written was dated September 23, 1770. He told how he could not preach although thousands were waiting to hear.

On September 29 he went from Portsmouth, New Hampshire, to Newbury, Massachusetts. He preached enroute in the open at Exeter, New Hampshire. Looking up he prayed,

> Lord Jesus, I am weary in thy work, but not of thy work. If I have not yet finished my course, let me go and speak for thee once more in the field, seal thy truth, and come home and die.

He was given strength for this his last sermon. The subject was *Faith and Works.* Although scarcely able to stand when he first came before the group, he preached for two hours to a crowd that no building then could have held.

Arriving at the parsonage of the First Presbyterian Church in Newburyport, which church he had helped to found, he had supper with his friend--Rev. Jonathan Parsons. He intended to go at once to bed. However, having heard of his arrival, a great number of friends gathered at the parsonage and begged him for just a short message. He paused a moment on the stairs, candle in hand, and spoke to the people as they stood listening until the candle went out. At 2 a.m. panting to breathe, he told his traveling companion Richard Smith, "My asthma is returning; I must have two or three days rest." His last words were, "I am dying" and at 6 a.m. on Sunday morning he died -- September 30, 1770.

The funeral was held on October 2 at the Old South First Presbyterian Church. Thousands of people were unable to even get near the door of the church. Whitefield had requested earlier to be buried beneath the pulpit if he died in that vicinity, which was done. Memorial services were held for him in many places.

John Wesley said:

> "Oh, what has the church suffered in the setting of that bright
> star which shone so gloriously in our hemisphere. We have
> none left to succeed him; none of his gifts; none of anything
> like him in usefulness."